KEYS FOR THE KINGDOM™
Theory and Technique
Level B

JOSEPH MARTIN

DAVID ANGERMAN

MARK HAYES

SOLE SELLING AGENT: SHAWNEE PRESS, INC., DELAWARE WATER GAP, PA 18327

H 5012

Foreword

This workbook is designed to provide reinforcement of the concepts the student is learning in *Keys for the Kingdom™, Level B.*

Included are exercises which help develop piano technique, activities which promote ear training and opportunities for the student to develop improvisational skills.

Together with its corresponding method book, *Theory and Technique, Level B* establishes foundations which assist the student in the creation of his or her own music and in the interpretation of the music of others with understanding, feeling and sensitive musicianship.

As is the case with all the supplemental books which are part of *Keys for the Kingdom™, Theory and Technique, Level B* is closely coordinated with the lessons in the matching method book.

Contents

V. I. P. Notes and Close Friends

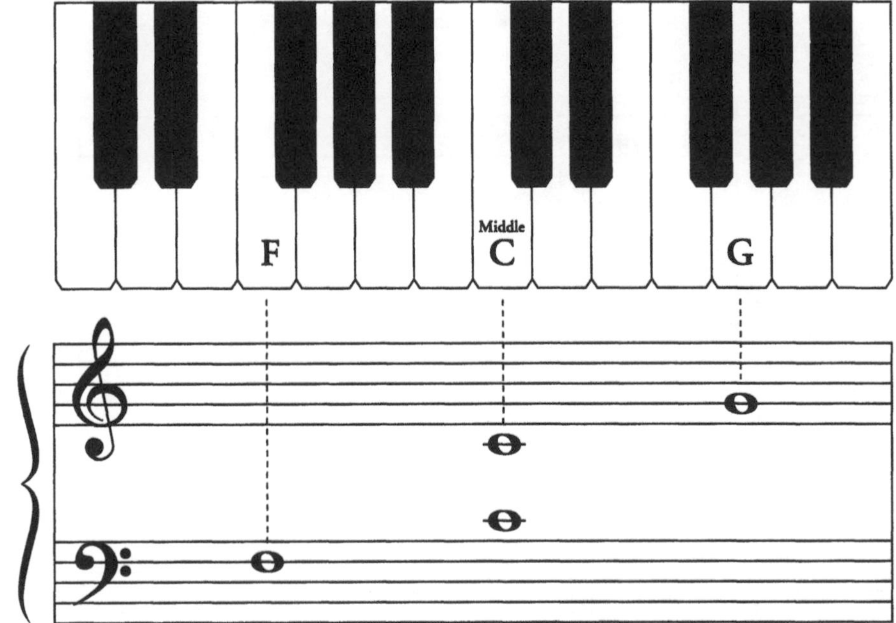

1. Circle and name the V. I. P. note, then name its close friends.

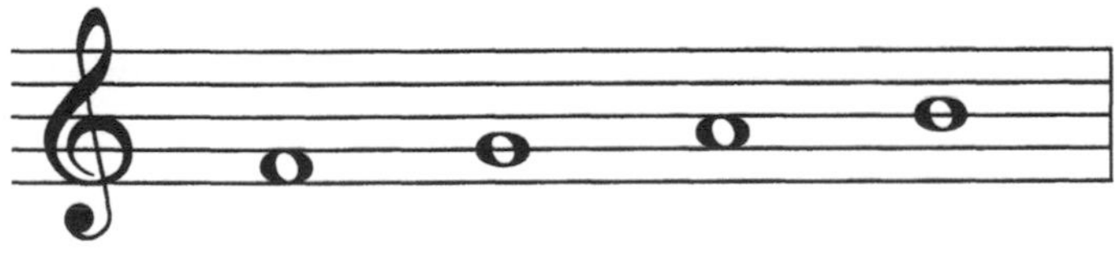

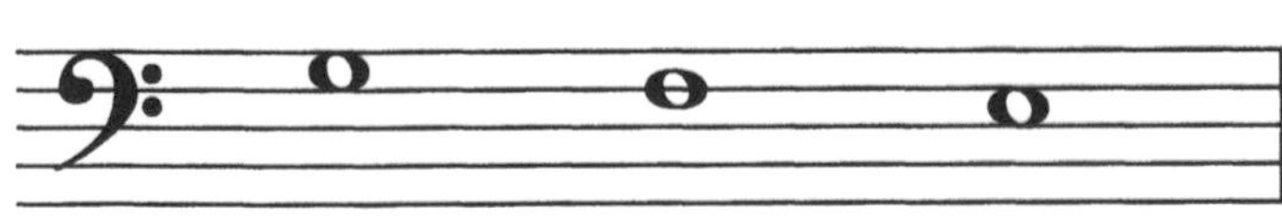

2. V. I. P. plus three! Draw three more notes in the direction of the arrow from each V. I. P. note. Play all four notes. Sing the letter names as you play.

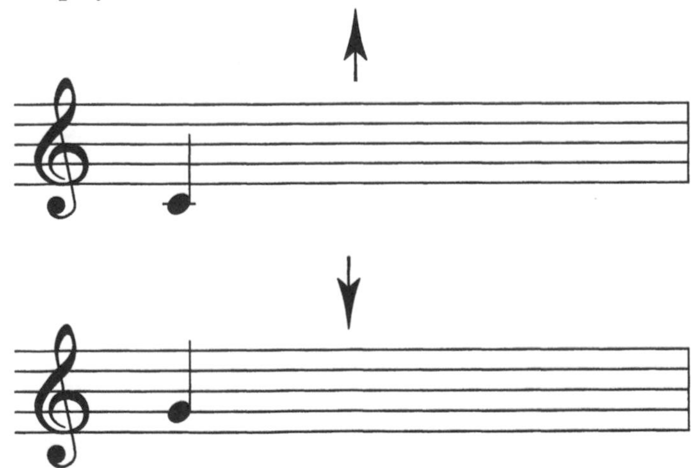

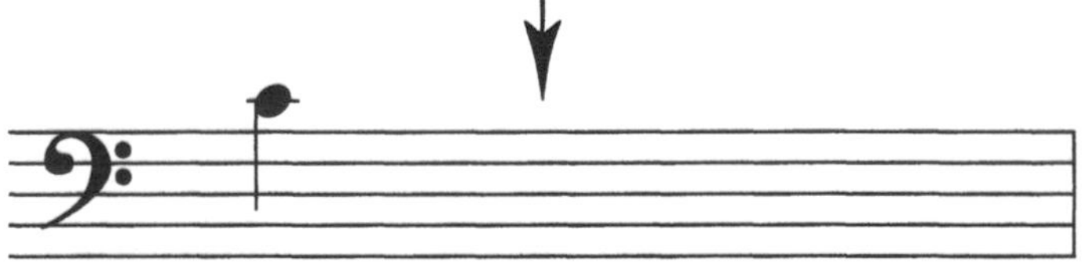

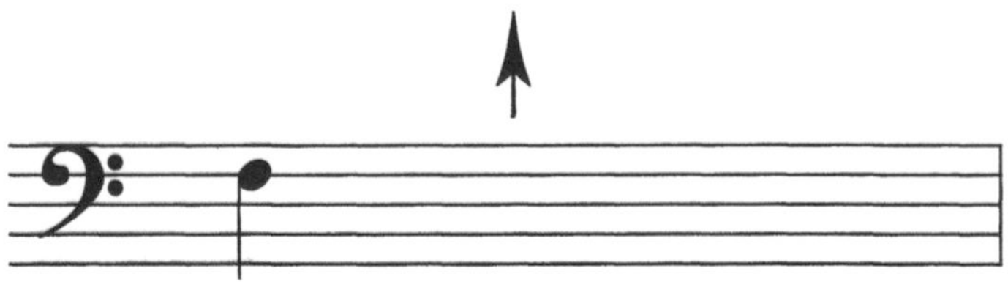

Use with pages 7 and 8 of Level B

Fingercize No. 1

1
f
p
3

f

Fingercize No. 2

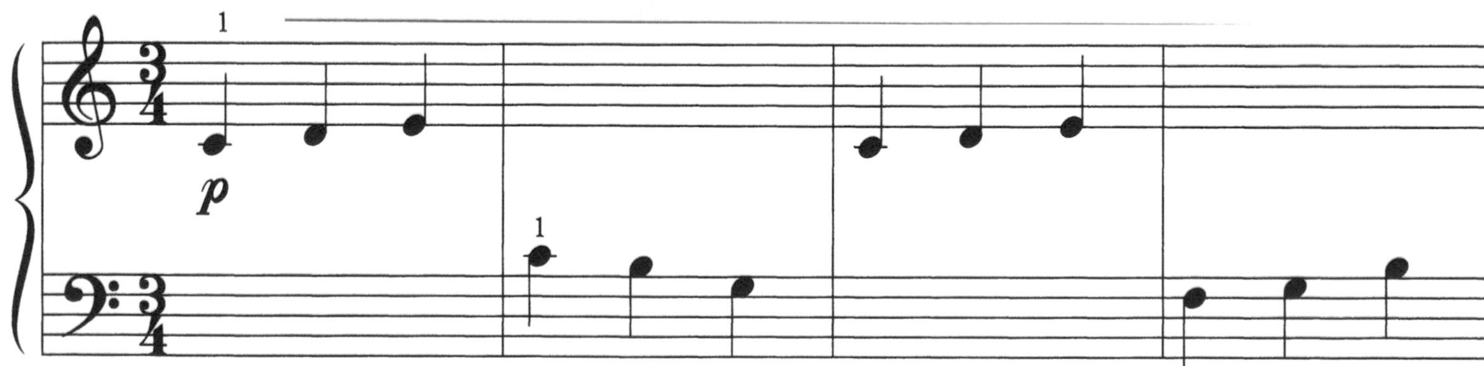
1
p
1

"C" manship

Ahoy, matey! Meet the new V. I. P. note, low C.

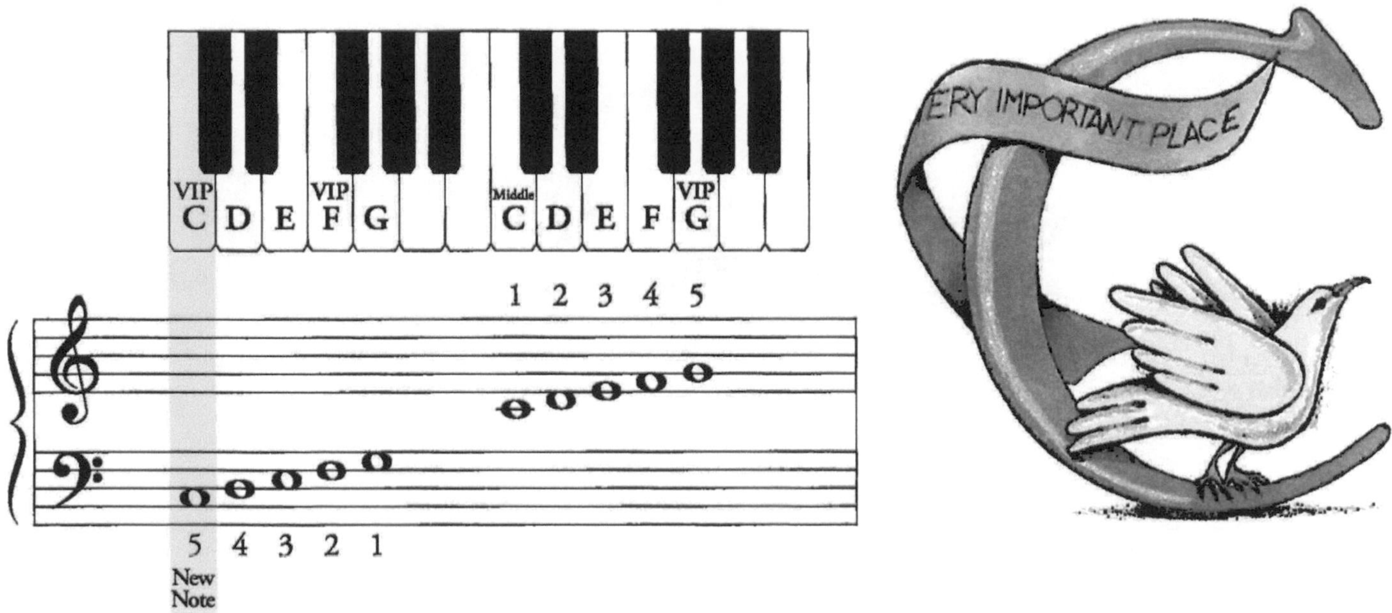

V. I. P. Stepper

Name each V. I. P. note. Then draw three more notes, stepping up or down from the V. I. P. Write their names in the spaces. Sing the letter names as you play.

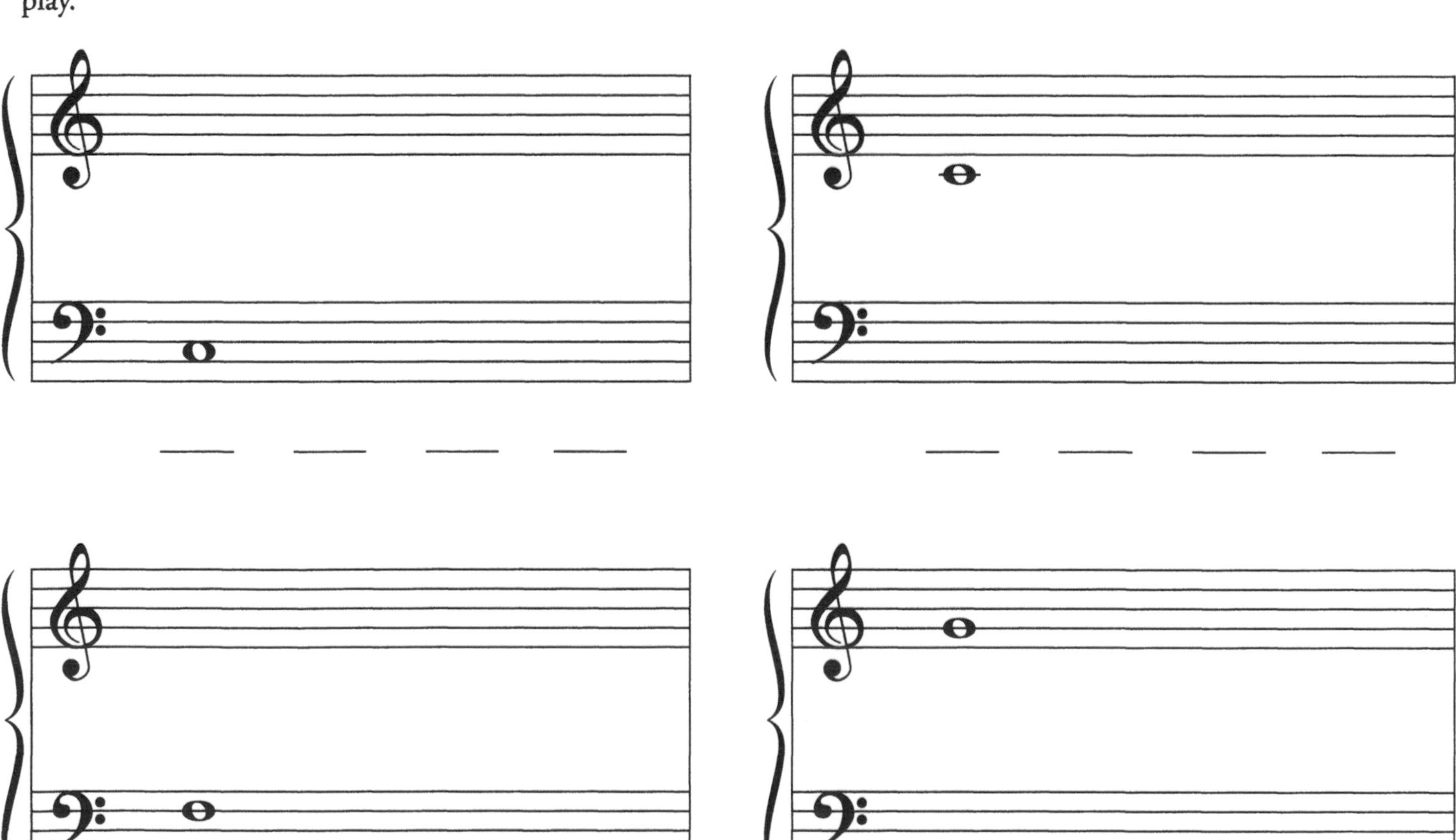

1. Circle all the "C" V. I. P. notes in the G and F clefs.
2. Sing the letter names as you play.
3. Count the rhythm as you play.
4. Sing the words as you play.

Deep Blue "C"

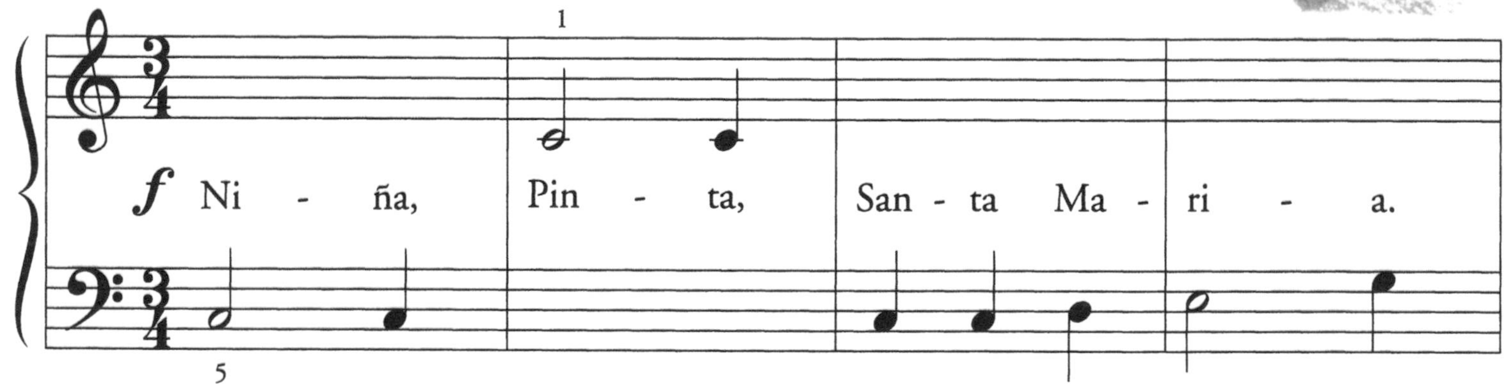

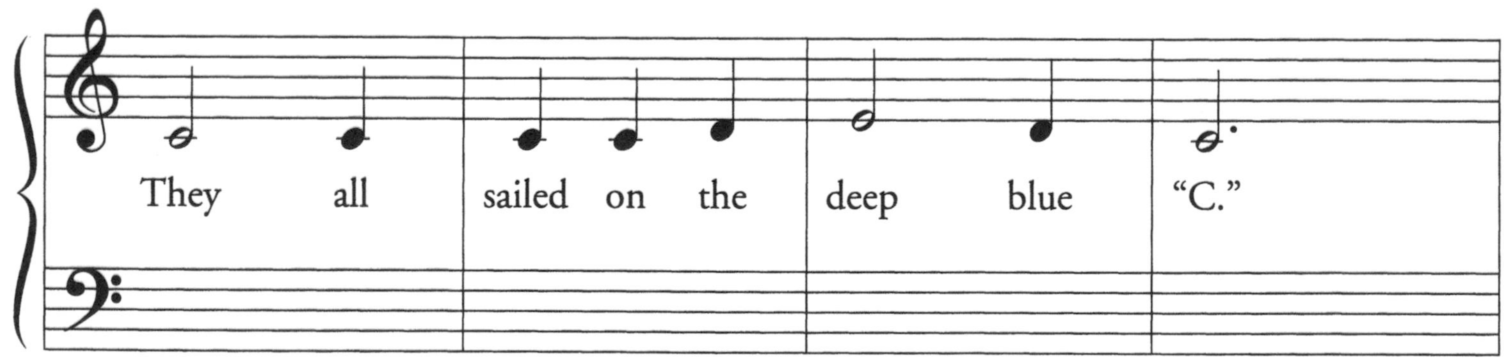

Whole Rest

A **rest** means silence in music.
A **whole rest** lasts for a whole measure.

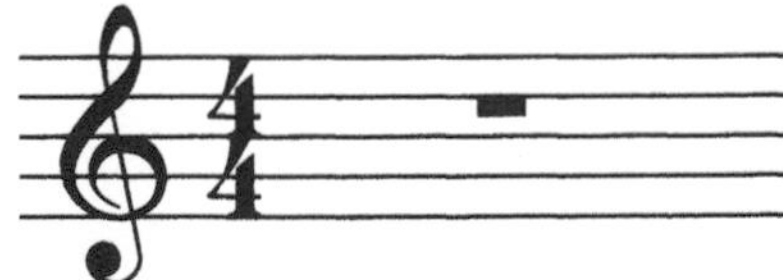

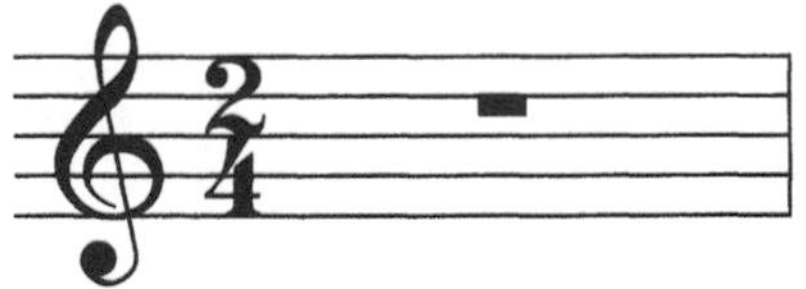

Check the time signature to see how many counts you will rest. Write the counts in the space. Then play each line, counting out loud as you play.

The Land of Rests

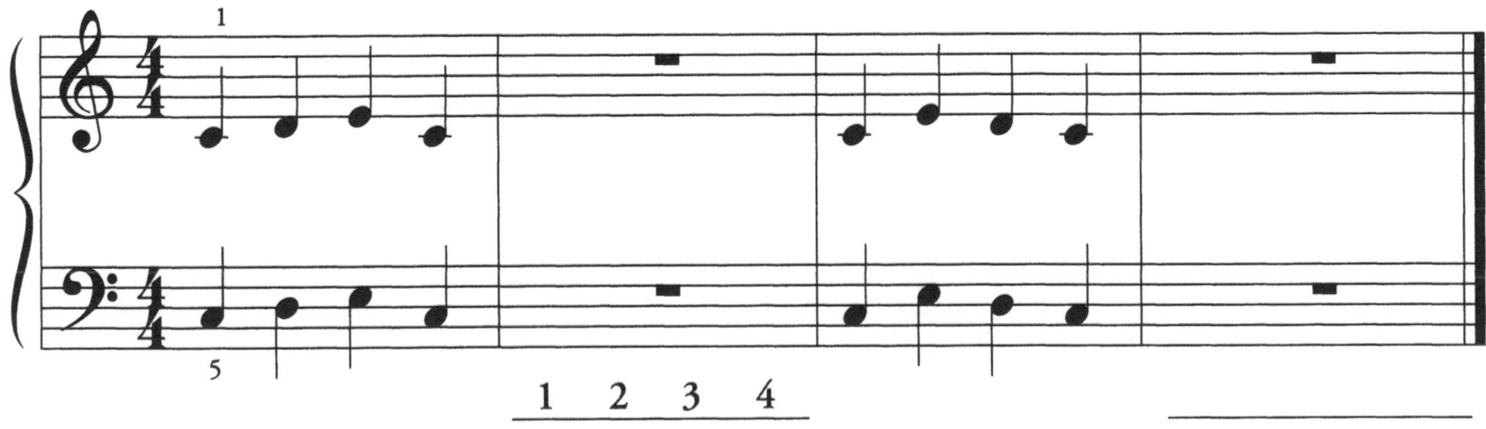

Give It a Rest

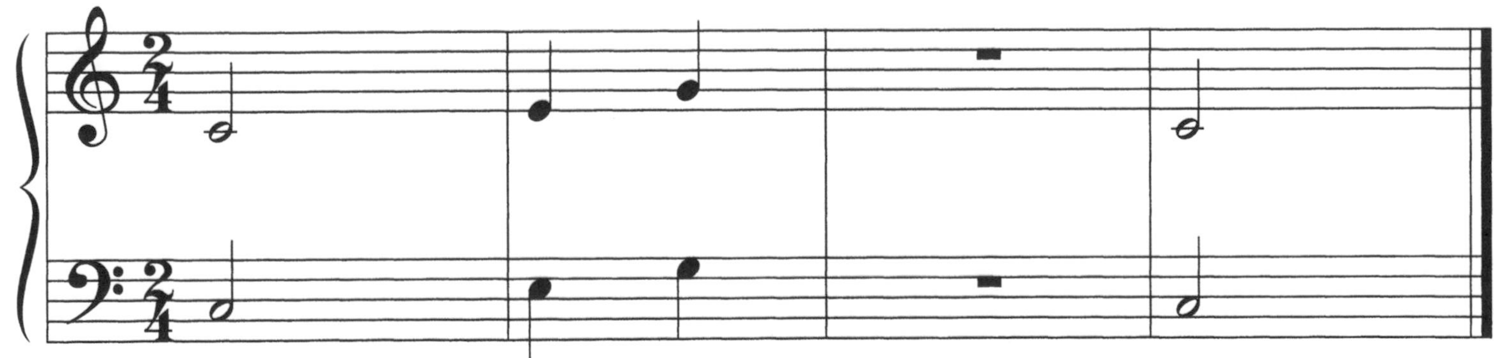

Red Light! Green Light!

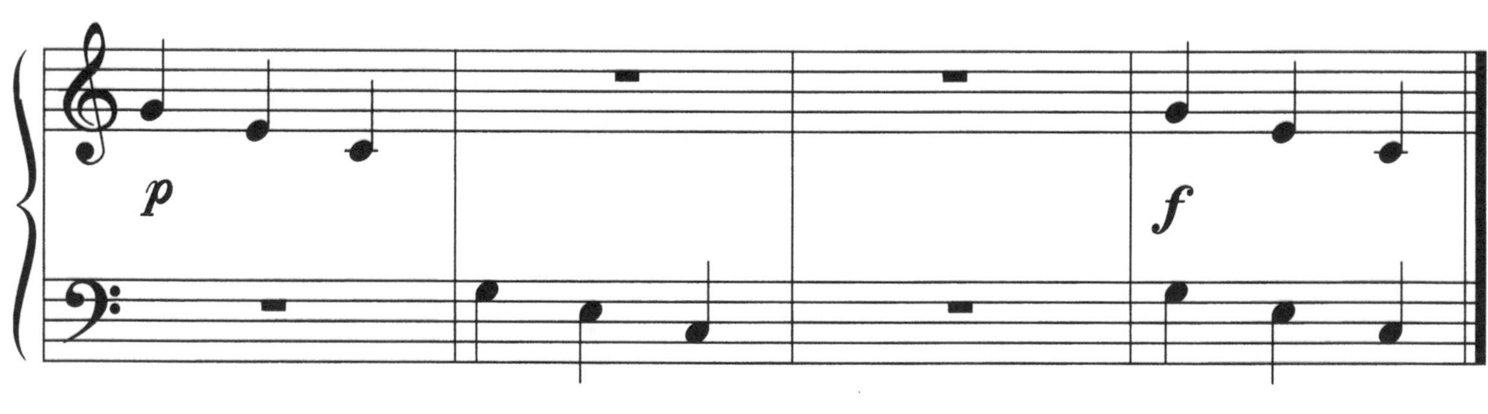

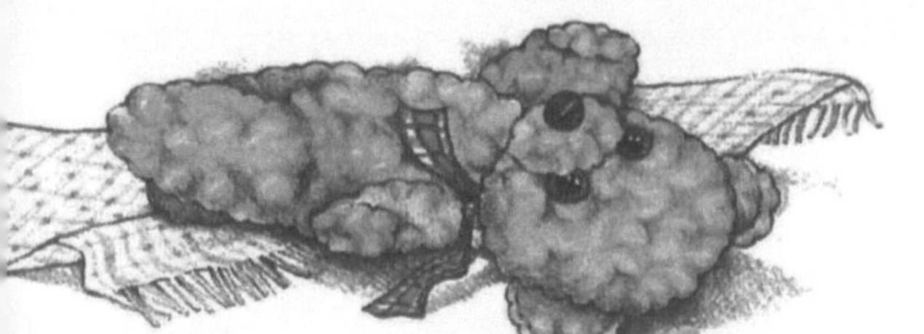

Use with pages 12 and 13 of Level B

FINGERCIZE NO. 3

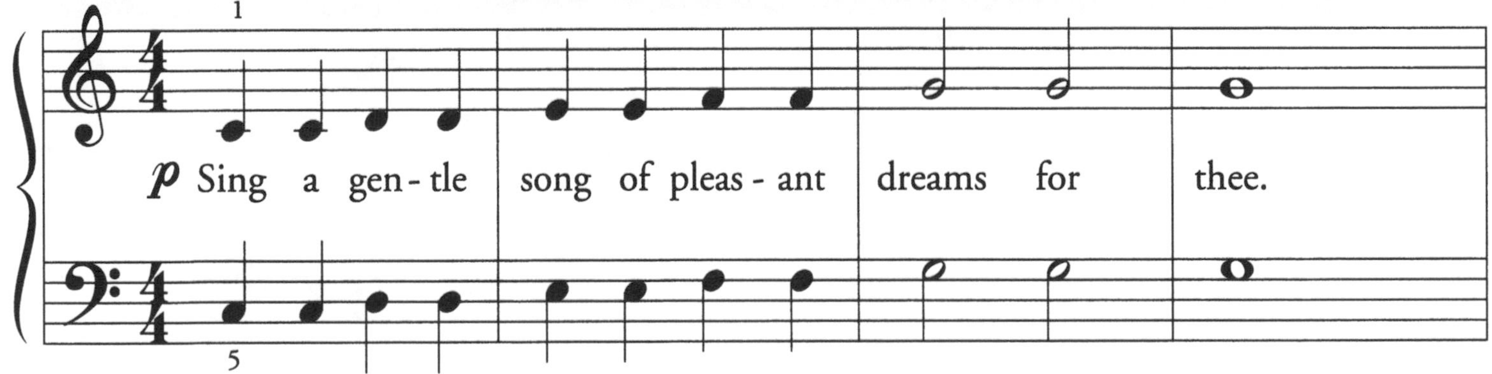
1
p Sing a gen - tle song of pleas - ant dreams for thee.
5

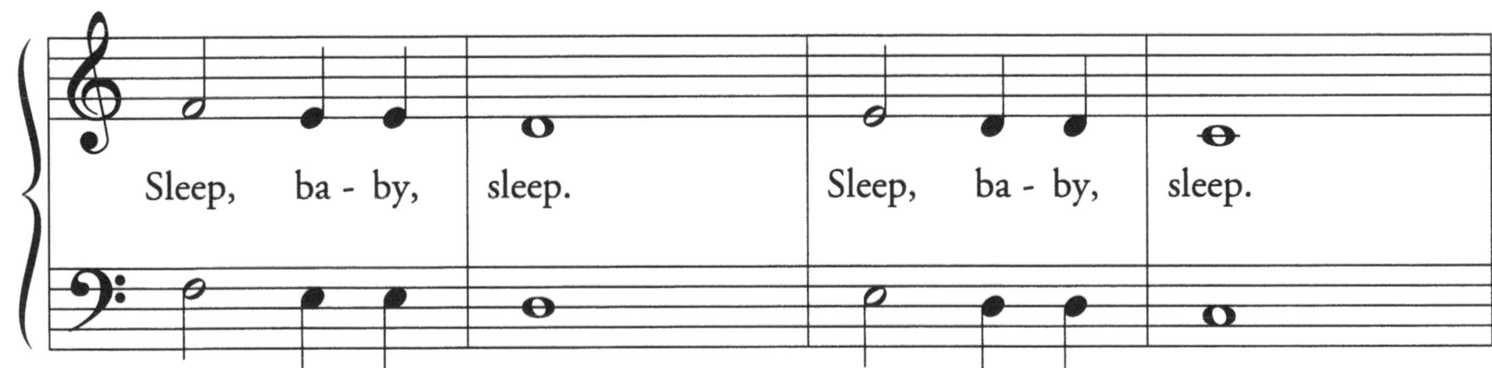
Sleep, ba - by, sleep. Sleep, ba - by, sleep.

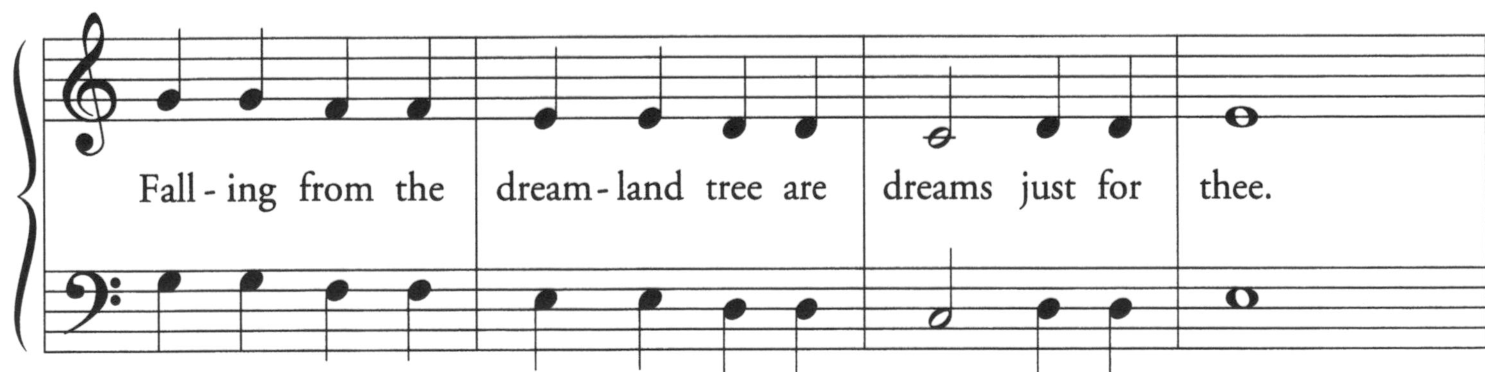
Fall - ing from the dream - land tree are dreams just for thee.

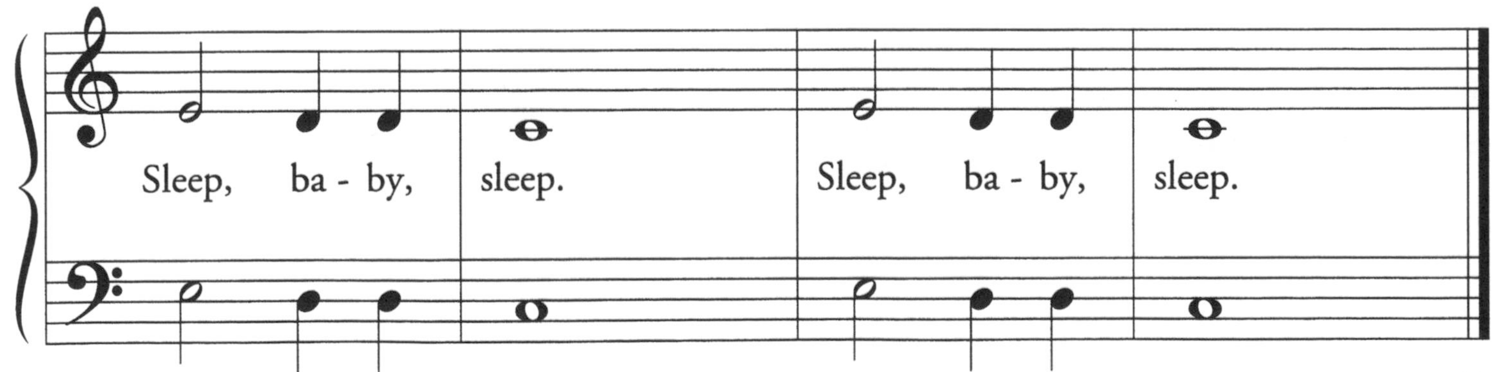
Sleep, ba - by, sleep. Sleep, ba - by, sleep.

Intervals—The Second

The distance from one note to another is called an **interval.**
A **2nd** is a step from a line to a space or from a space to a line.

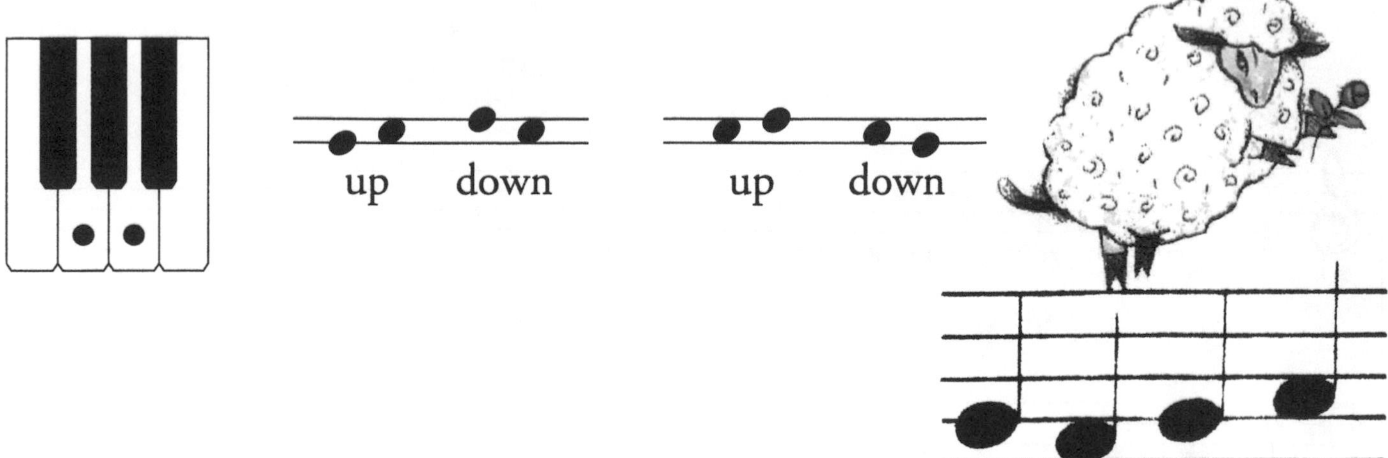

1. Find and mark each 2nd.

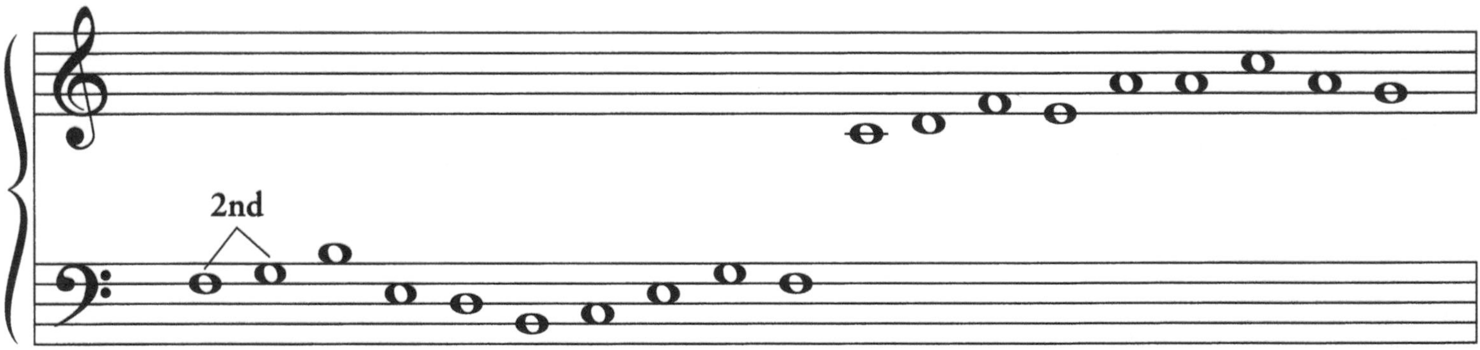

2. Draw a note a 2nd above or below each note in the direction of the arrow.

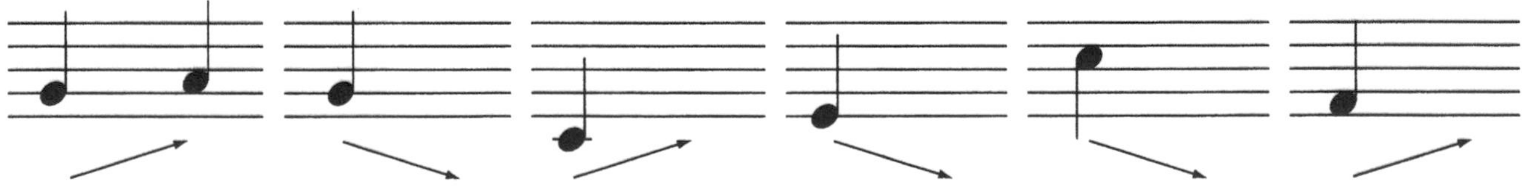

3. Find and mark all the 2nds on the keyboard.

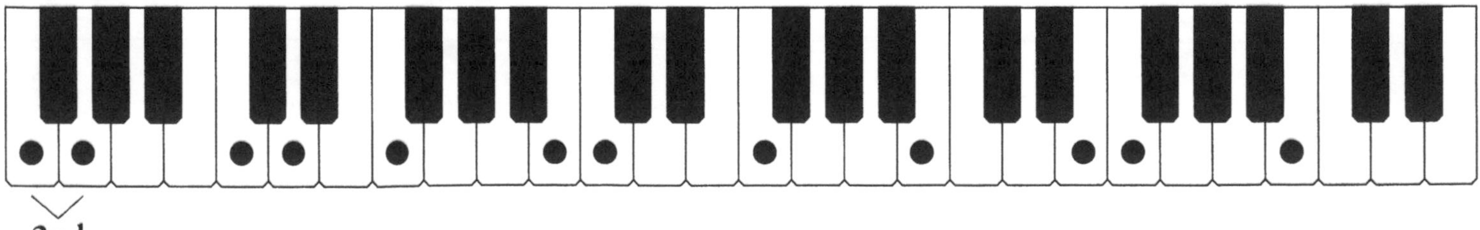

4. Name the key a 2nd **above** each named key.

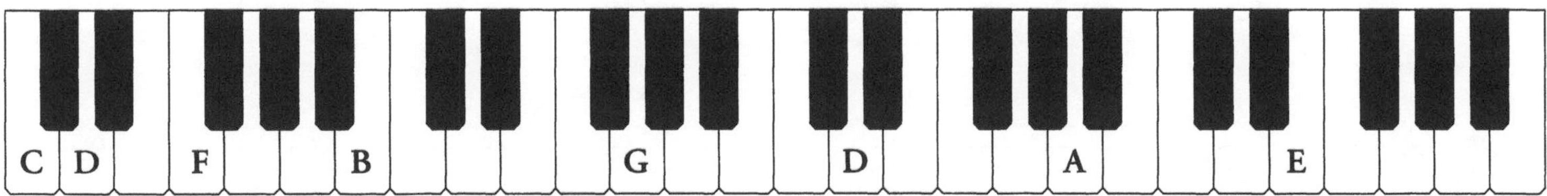

5. Name the key a 2nd **below** each named key.

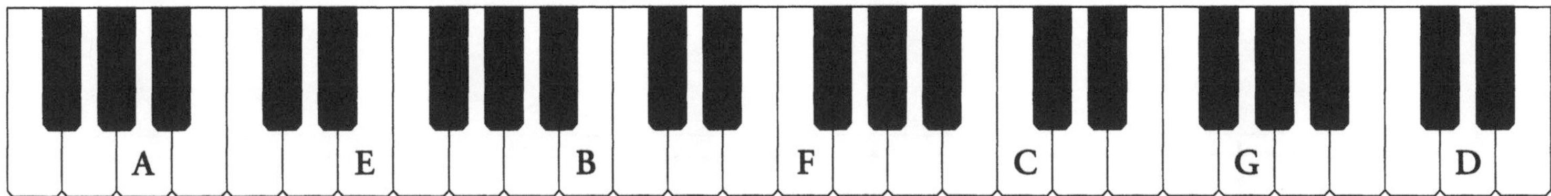

6. On each staff, draw two more notes in 2nds in the direction of the arrow from each starting note. Write the names of the notes on the keyboard.

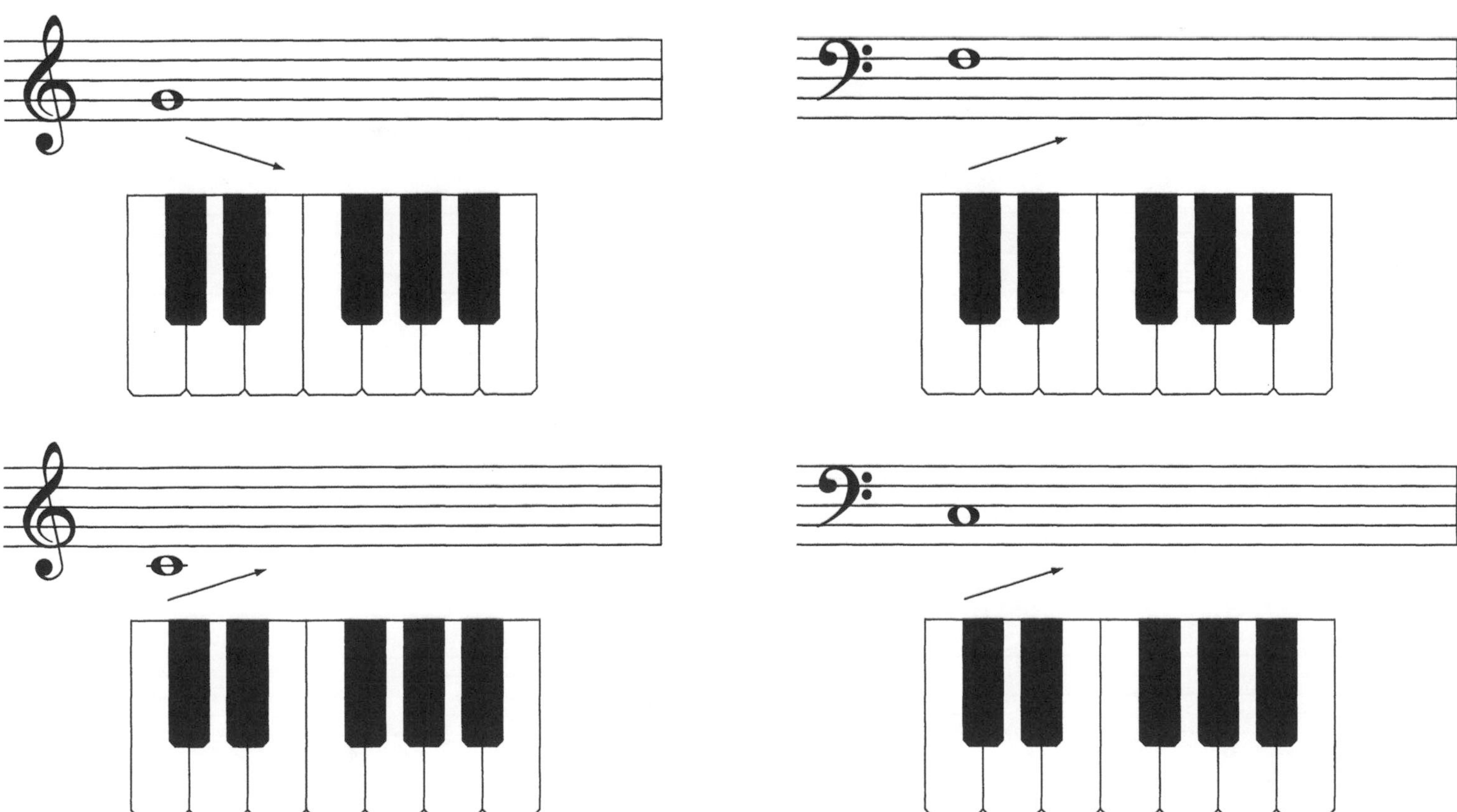

Fingercize No. 4

Fingercize No. 5

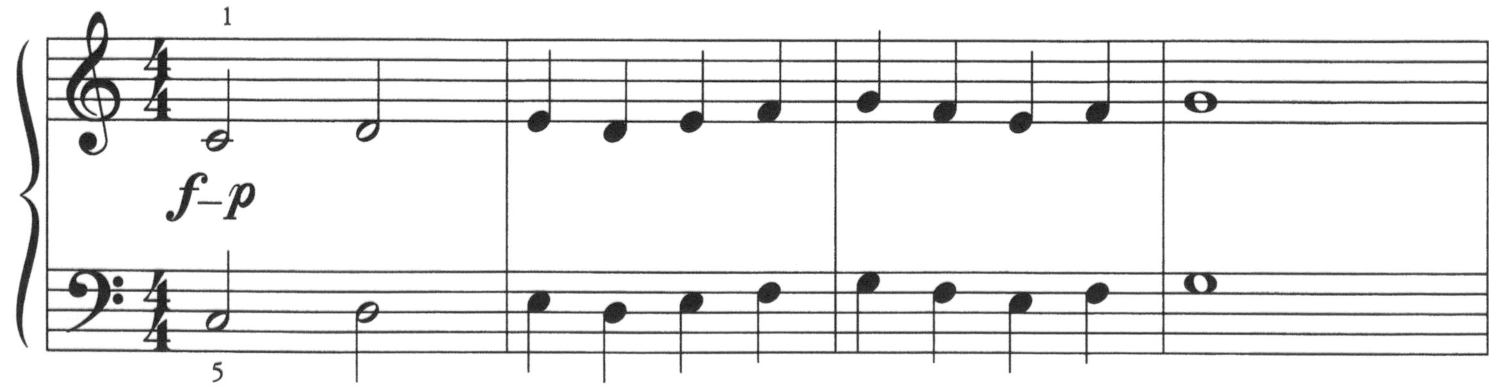

Intervals—The Third

The interval of a **3rd** skips one key or note.
A 3rd is a skip from a line to a line or from a space to a space.

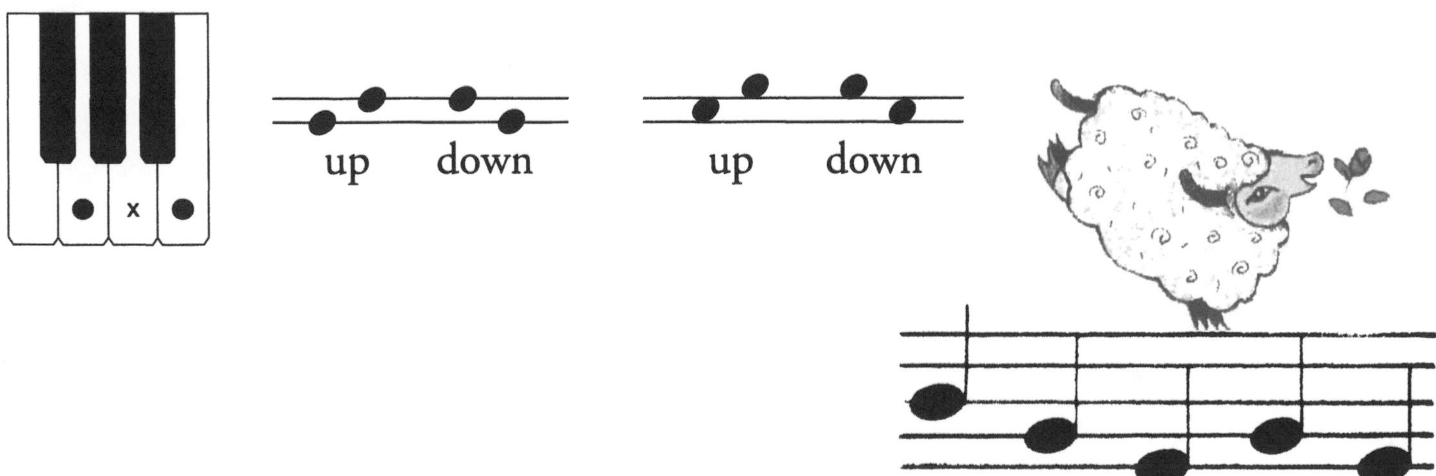

1. Find and mark each 3rd.

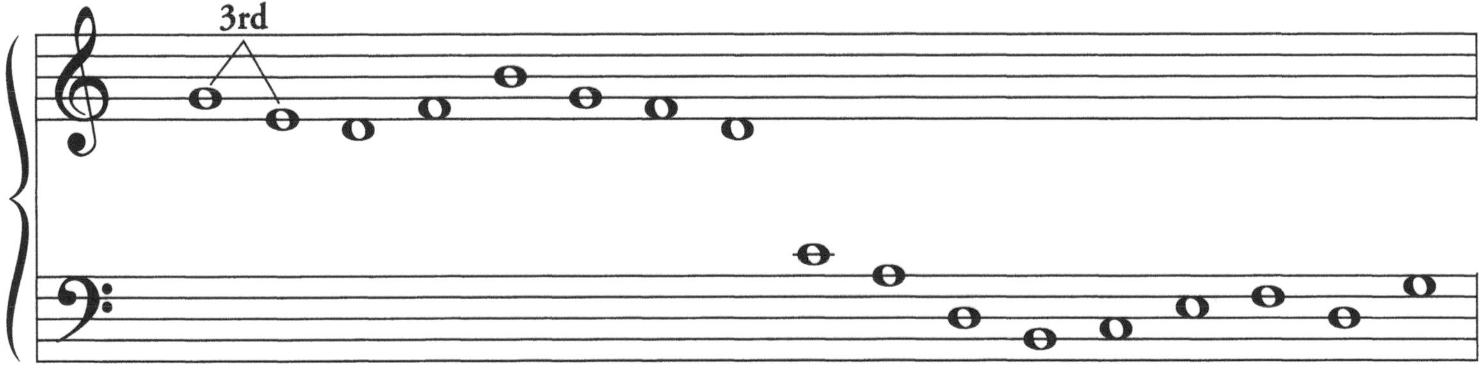

2. Draw a note a 3rd above or below each note in the direction of the arrow.

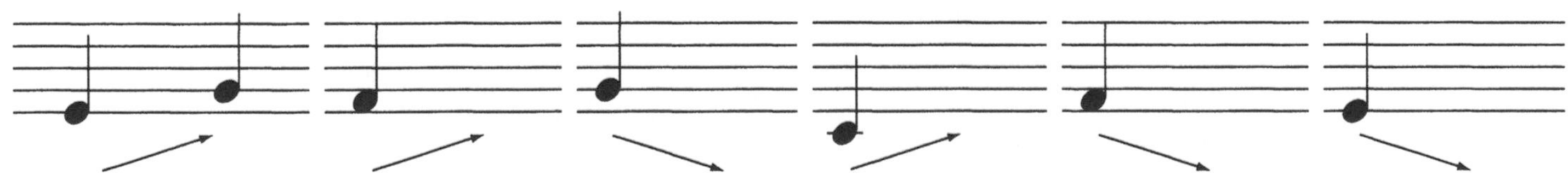

3. Find and mark all the 3rds on the keyboard.

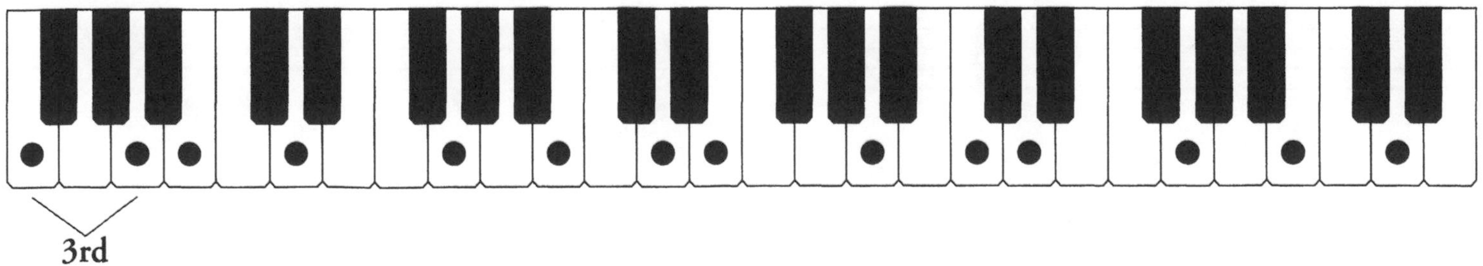

Quarter Rest

A quarter rest gets one beat just like a quarter note.

1. Count out loud as you play. Say "rest" for each quarter rest.

2. Draw quarter rests to make the correct number of beats in each measure.
   Play and count. Say "rest" for each quarter rest.

Lose Wait!

Each example has too many rests. Cross out rests to get the correct number of beats for each measure. Be sure to check the time signature.

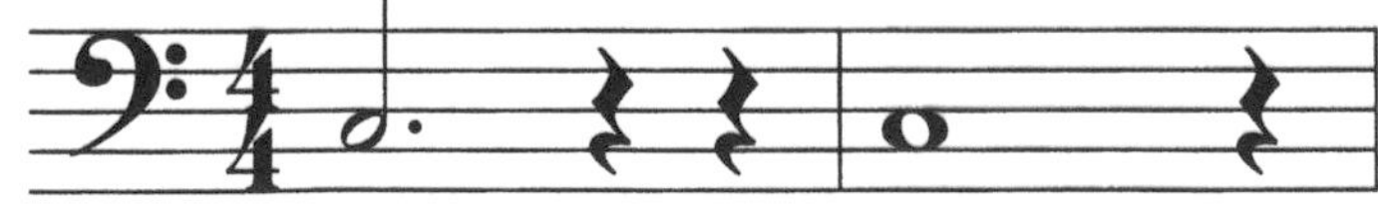

Practice Directions

1. Play *Fingercize No. 6* and sing the letter names.
2. Play and count the rhythm. Say "rest" for each quarter note.

IMAGINATION DESTINATION

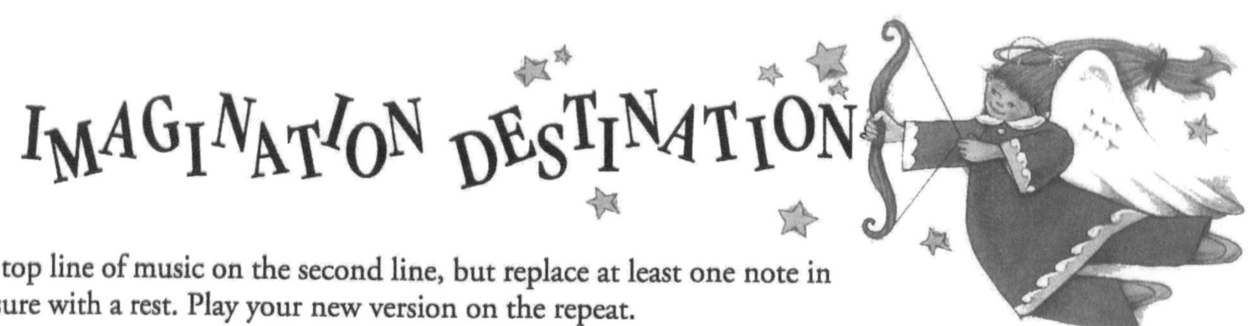

Copy the top line of music on the second line, but replace at least one note in each measure with a rest. Play your new version on the repeat.

Restin' Piece

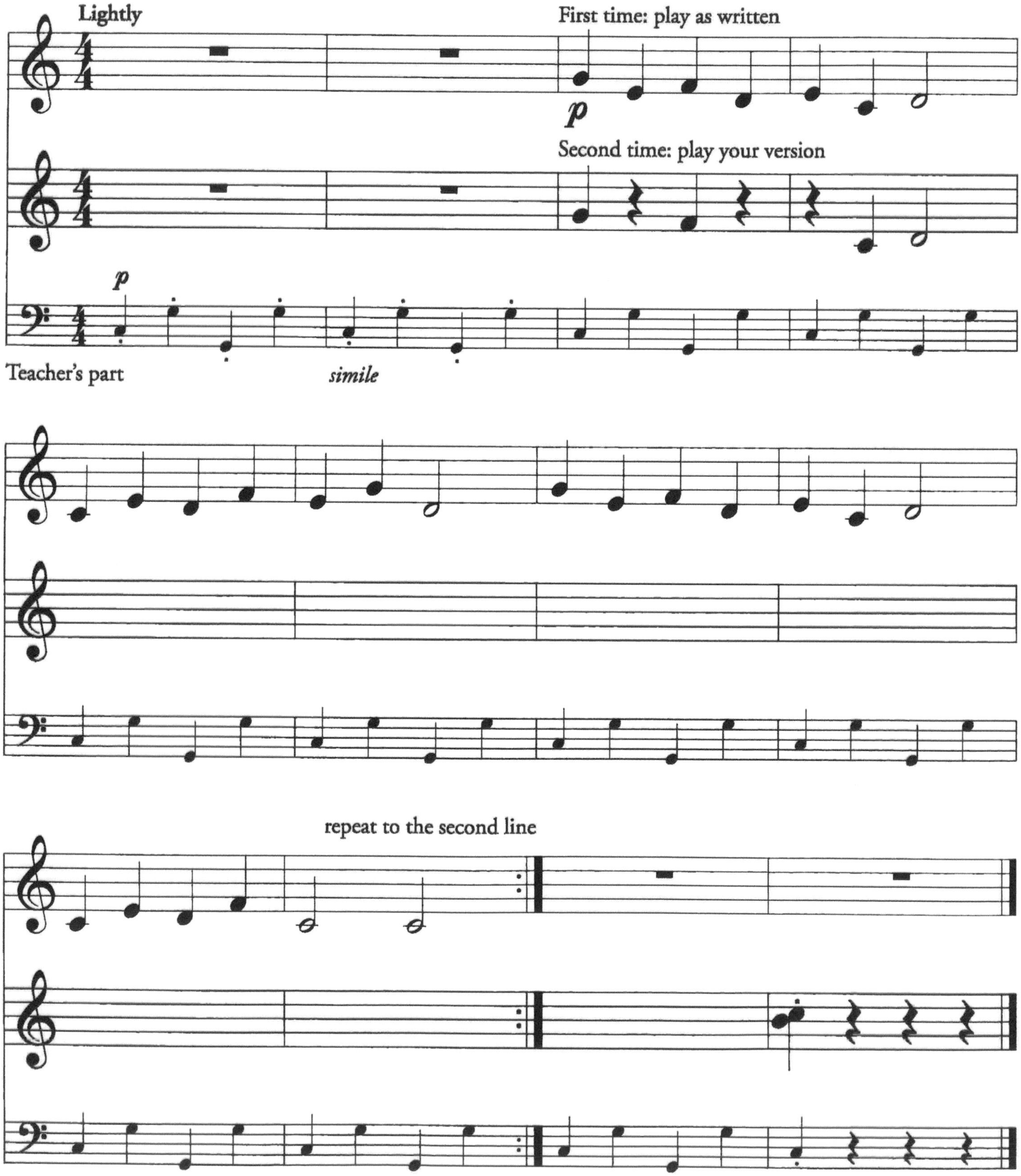

Lightly
First time: play as written
p
Second time: play your version
p
Teacher's part
simile
repeat to the second line

The Slur

The **slur** is a curved line over or under two or more different notes. Notes that are slurred should be played smoothly connected (*legato*).

Play the melody below. Play *legato* or connected through each slur. Lift your hand at the end of each slur, leading up with your wrist.

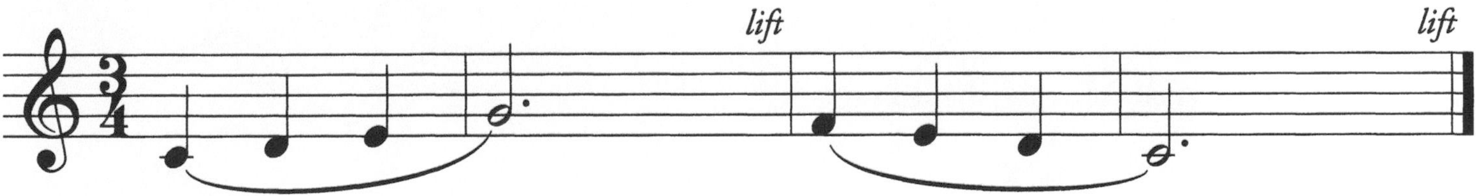

Music Composer!

Help finish the song by adding…

notes	words
rests	brace at the beginnning of each line
slurs	double bar at the end
dynamics (*f* or *p*)	fingering

Melodic and Harmonic Intervals

Melodic intervals are notes played **separately** as in a melody.

melodic 2nd:   melodic 3rd: 

Harmonic intervals are notes played **at the same time.**

harmonic 2nd: 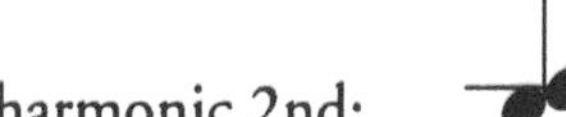 harmonic 3rd:  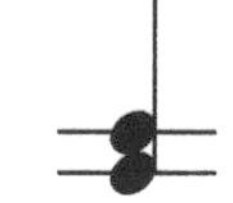

Harmonizer!

1. Rewrite the melodic intervals as harmonic intervals. Use half notes.
2. Play each example.

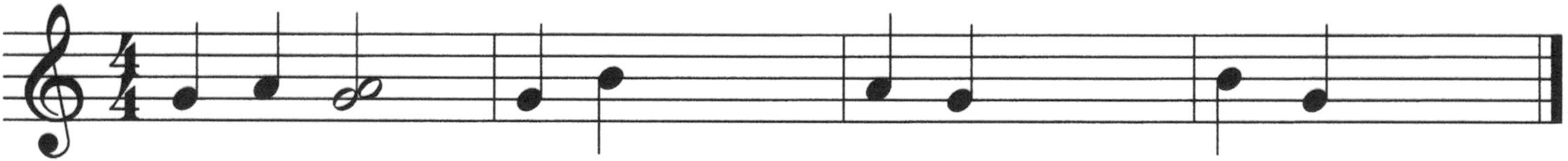

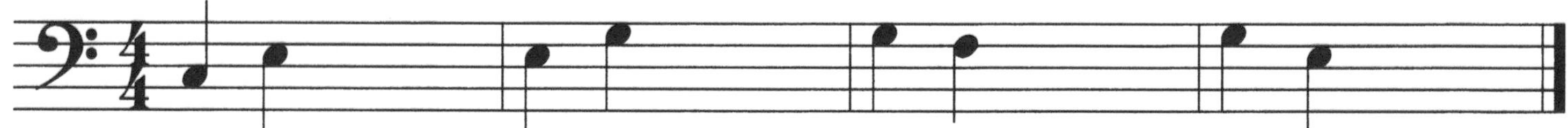

De-Harmonizer!

1. Rewrite the harmonic intervals as melodic intervals. Use quarter notes.
2. Play each example.

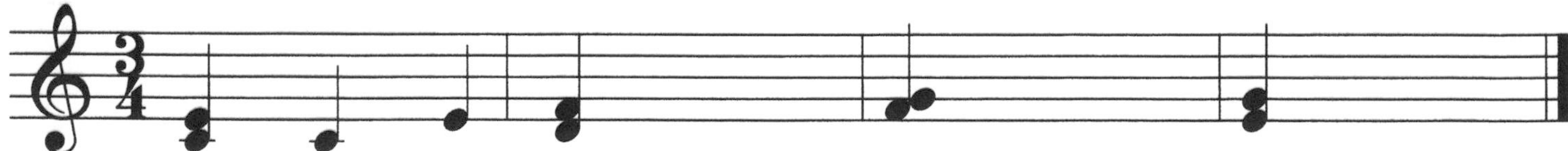

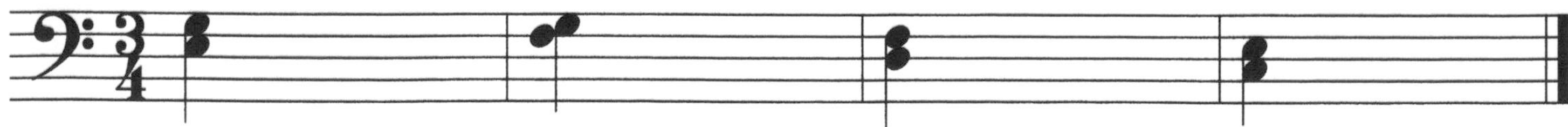

More New Notes

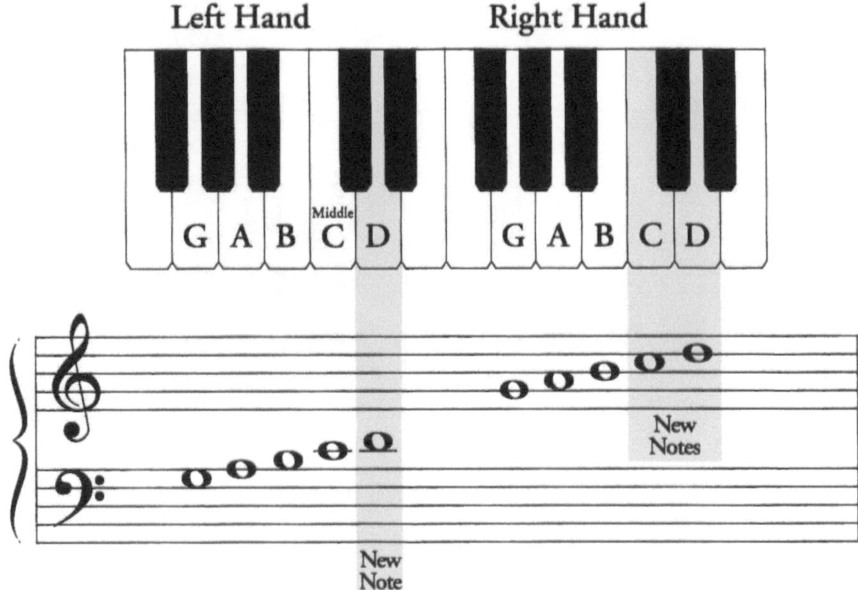

Interval Training

1. Write the correct melodic interval from the starting note.
2. Name both notes. Play.

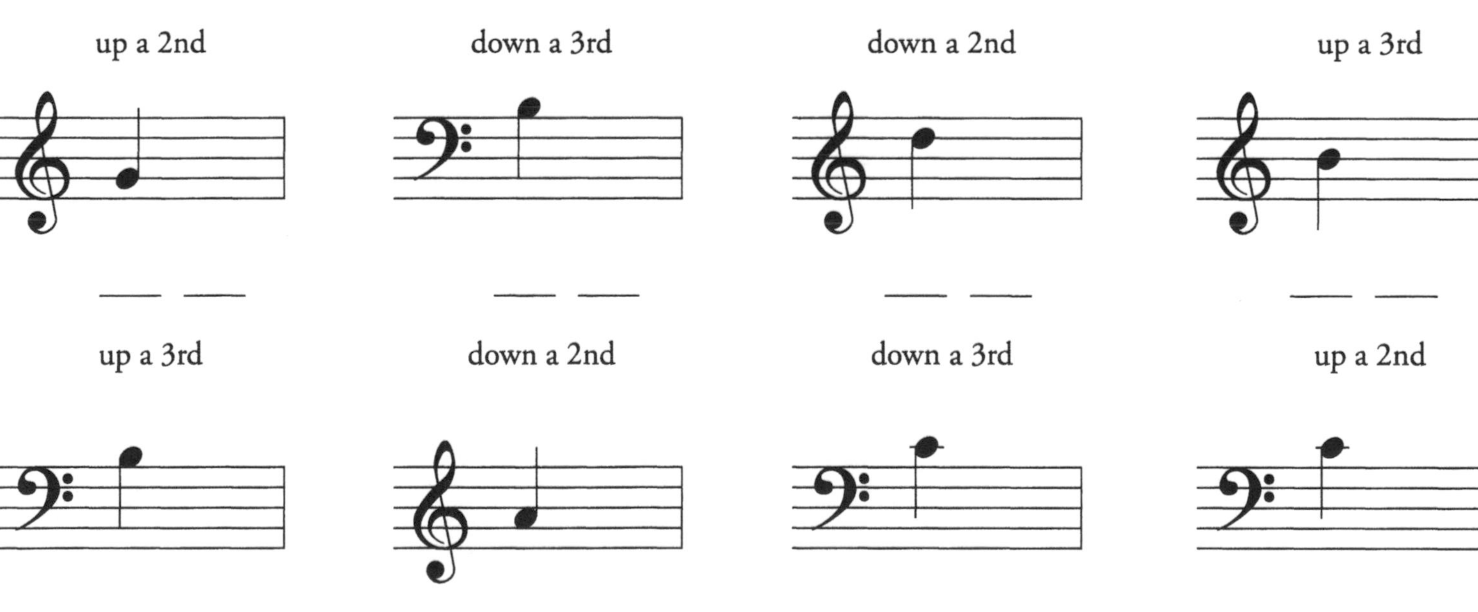

3. Name the harmonic interval. Then name each note.

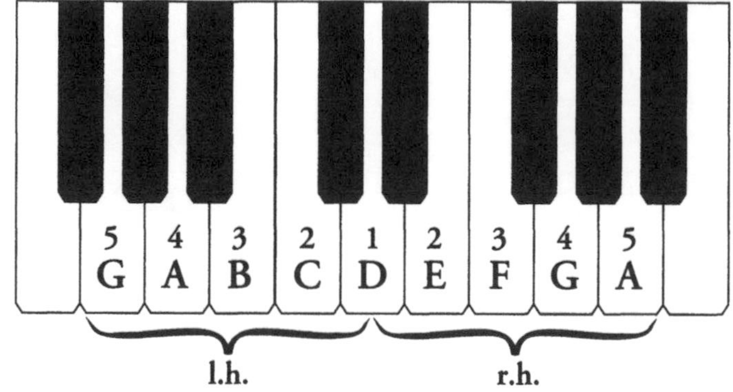

First, write step, skip, or repeat in the boxes (measures) provided:

4/4

r.h.	l.h.	r.h.	l.h.
skip	______	______	______

r.h.	l.h.	r.h.	r.h.
______	______	______	______

Then, as your teacher plays, make up your own melody based on the patterns you have chosen. As you gain confidence, add new rhythms and dynamics for variety.

Note to Teacher: As a variation, *verbally* call out step, skip or repeat for your student to follow in improvising.

The Royal "Diad"em

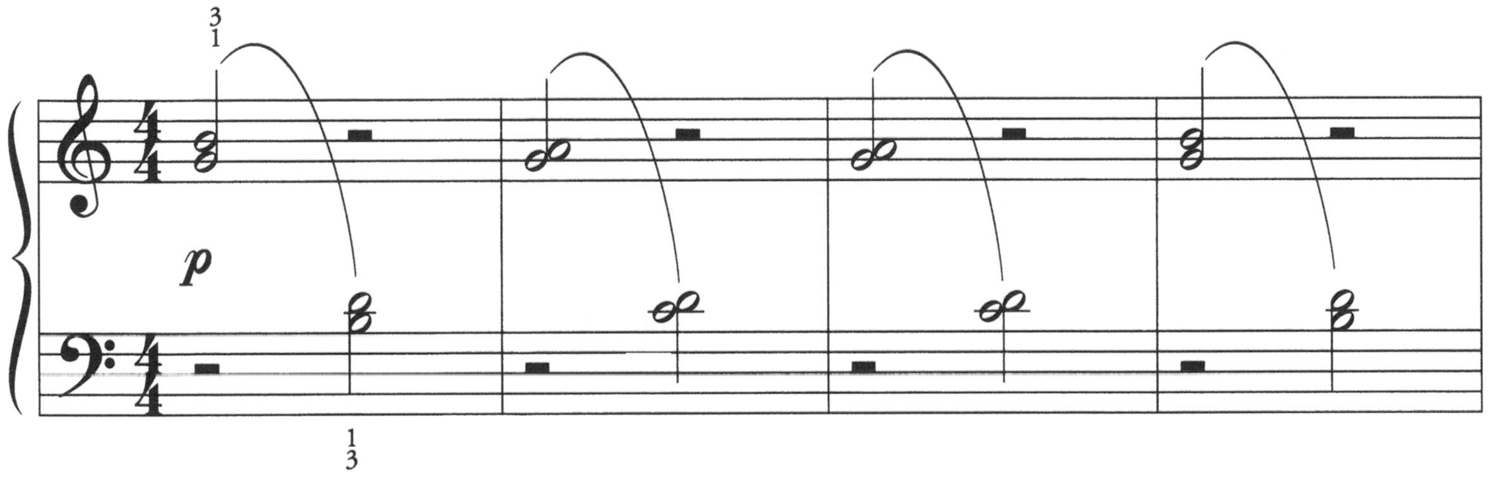

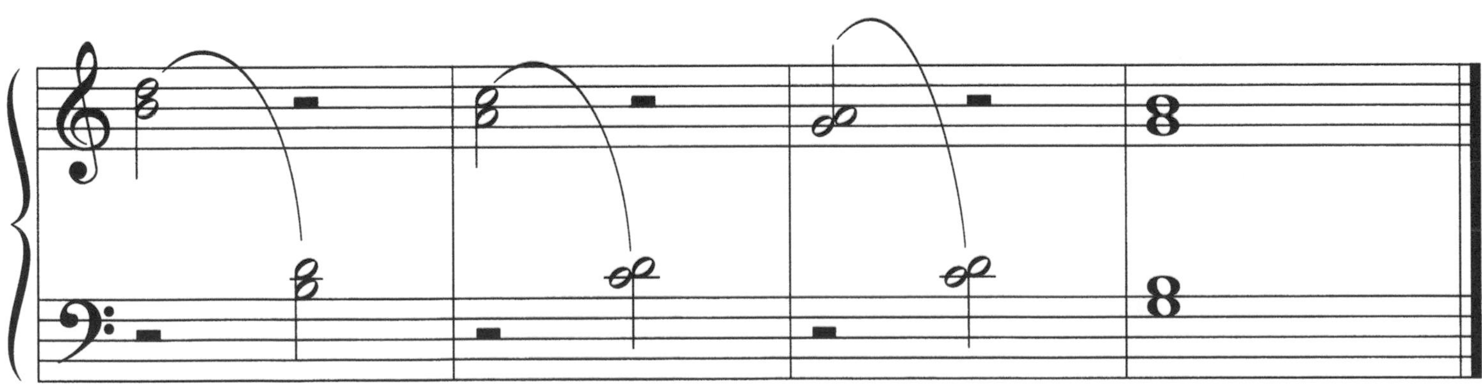

D. C. Is Tops!

D. C. stands for ***da capo.*** In Italian it means "the cap" or "the top." The Italian word for the finish is ***fine,*** pronounced "fee-nay."
D. C. al fine means go back to the beginning (or the top) and play to the end (or finish).
The sign, ***D. C. al fine,*** is used when the first part of a song is repeated at the end. Instead of writing the music all over again, the composer uses the sign ***D. C. al fine.***

1. Play *My Best Friend Is Jesus.* Notice that the first and third lines are alike.

1. My Best Friend Is Jesus

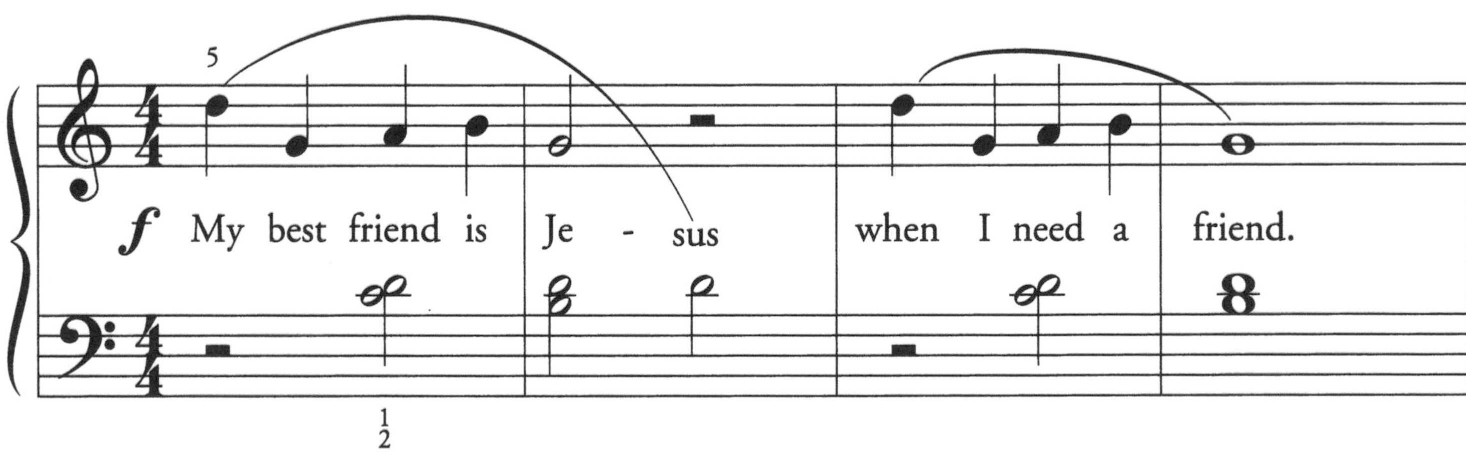

2. Play version two of *My Best Friend Is Jesus.* Be sure to follow the *D. C. al fine* sign.

2. My Best Friend Is Jesus

(version two with D. C. al fine)

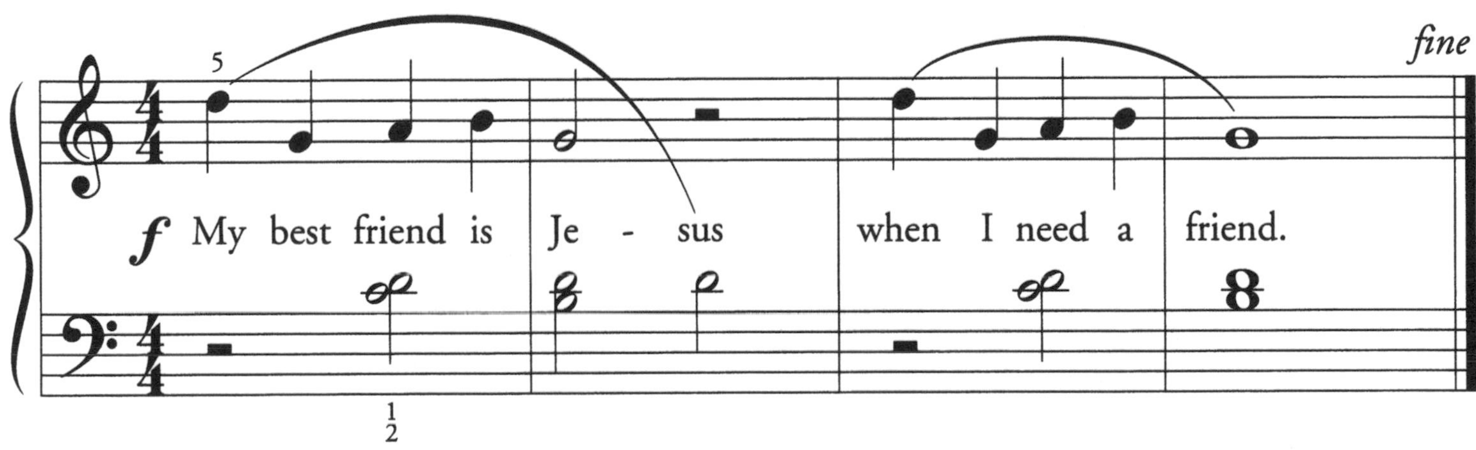

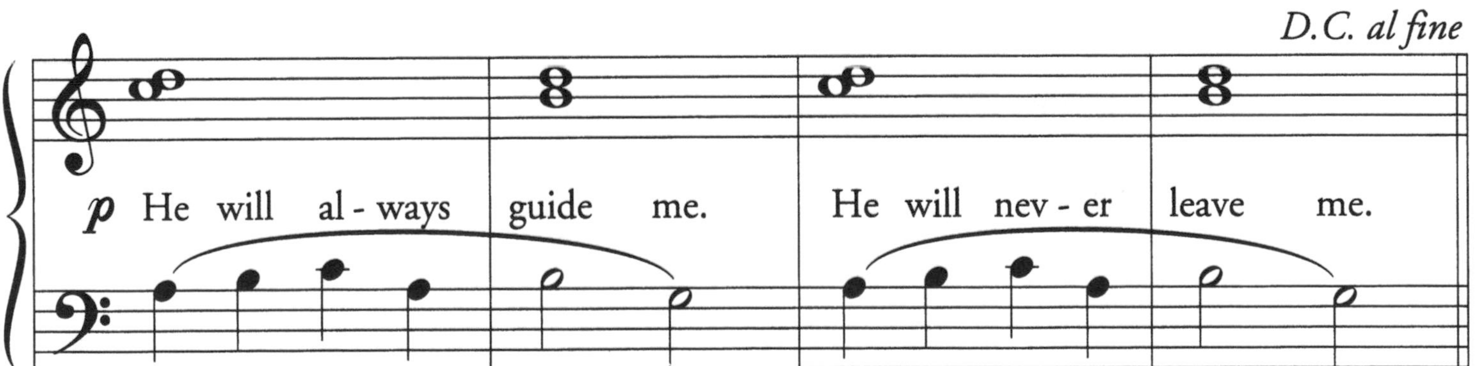

Intervals—The Fourth

The interval of a **4th** skips two keys or notes.

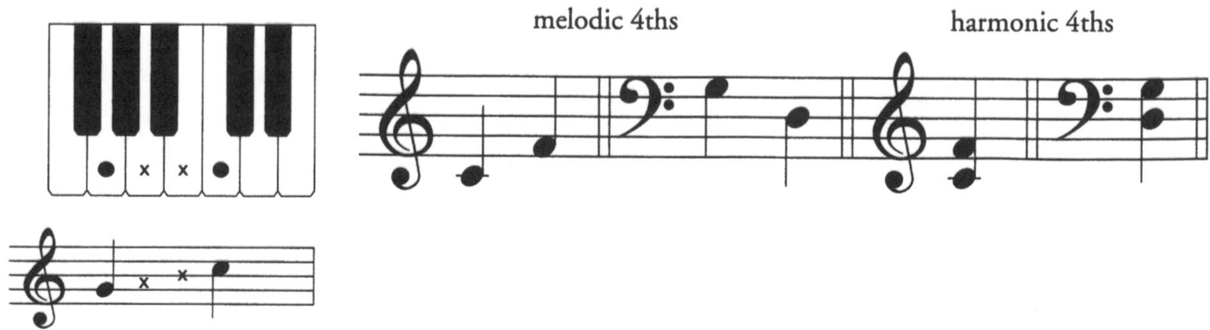

4th Factory

This factory is trying to make only 4ths.

1. Draw an X through any intervals that are not 4ths.

2. Show them how it's done! Draw a note a melodic 4th in the direction of the arrow.

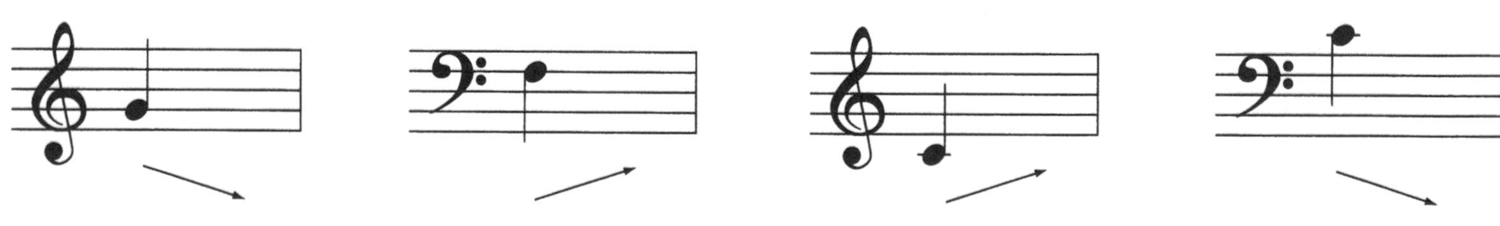

3. Write in the letter name of the note a 4th in the direction of the arrow.

4. Name the harmonic interval and each note.

Fingercize No. 7

1 4

f–p

5 2

Practice Directions

1. Play *High-Low* and sing the letter names.
2. Sing the words as you play.
3. Now, play and leave out the note on all the "Lows" each time. Think the word, but don't say it out loud. You are putting a quarter rest in place of the "low."

High-Low

4 1

f High, low, high, low, | high, low, high, low, | high, low, high, low, | high, low, high, low,

2 5

high, low, high, low, | high, low, high, low, | high, low, high, low, | high, low, high.

The Tie

The tie is a curved line that connects two neighboring notes of the same pitch. When two notes are tied, they sound as one note. Play the first note, then count the value of both notes. Hold through the second note.

Ties Across the Bar Line

1. Ties usually cross bar lines. Add the values of the two tied notes and fill in the correct number of beats.
2. Draw the bar line between the correct beats to match the tied notes.

3. Play each line below without ties.
4. Draw in the dotted ties. Play each line with ties.

1. Find and circle the tied notes in the song *Blest Be the Tie.*
2. Sing the letter names as you play.
3. Count the rhythm as you play.

Blest Be the Tie

Words by John Fawcett (1740–1817)

Music by Johann G. Nägeli (1773–1836)

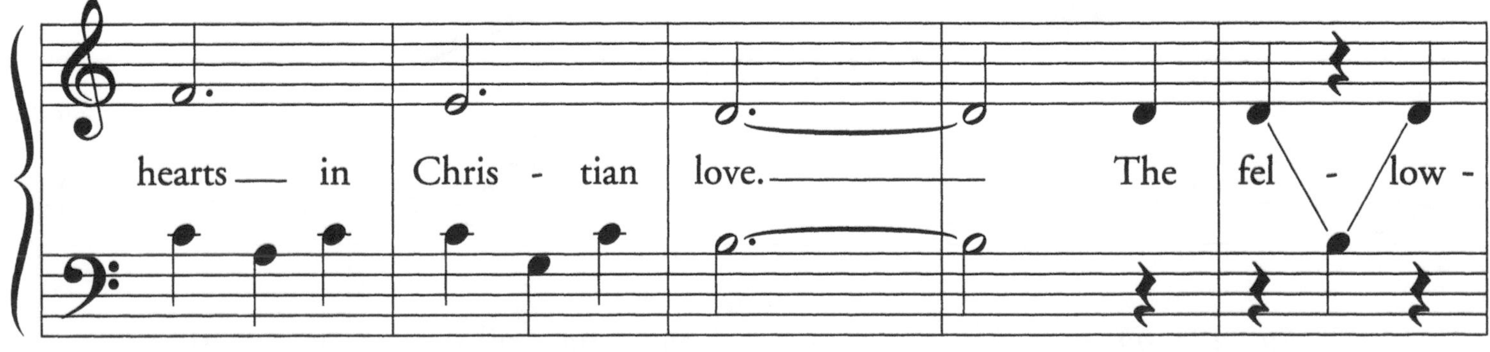

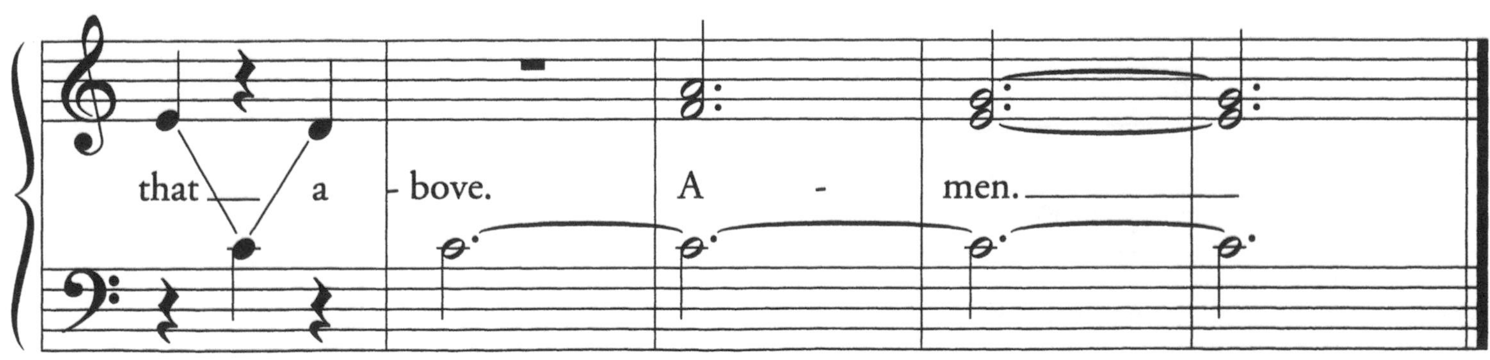

Sailing on the High "C"s

Hoist the anchor! Set the sails and stand fast! We're headed for the high C!
V. I. P. Cs, that is.

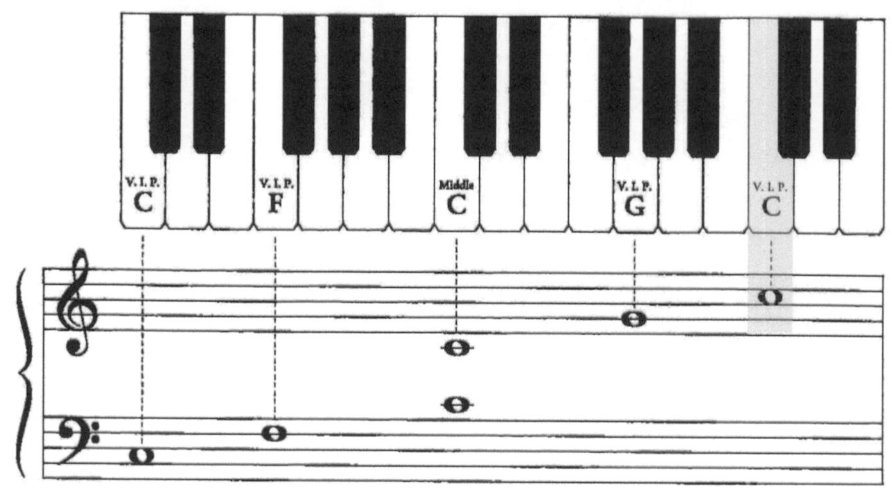

1. In *"C" Chantey Shuffle,* find and circle the first V. I. P. C note in each phrase.
2. Play.

*There are actually eight Cs on the full keyboard.

Accent (<)

Accent means to play a note with a sudden strong touch. Accents are just above or below the note head.

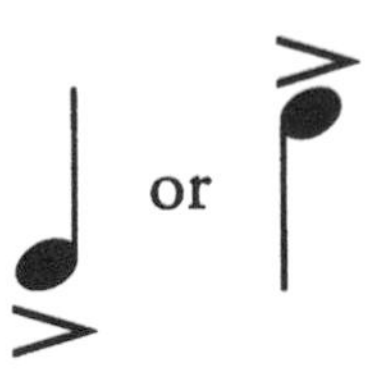

Play *Northern Accent.* Be sure to accent only the notes that are marked with a <.

What other melody do you hear? ____________________

Interval Train Depot

Discover the letter name of each train. Start with the note name on the caboose and work your way to the engine. Put the letter name of the train on the engine.

Intervals—The Fifth

The interval of a 5th skips three keys or notes.

Getting to Know 5ths

1. Find the 5ths. Draw a circle around the melodic 5ths and a square around the harmonic 5ths.

2. Draw a note a harmonic 5th below each note. Name both notes.

3. Hop up the keyboard by 5ths. Write in the letter name at each hop.

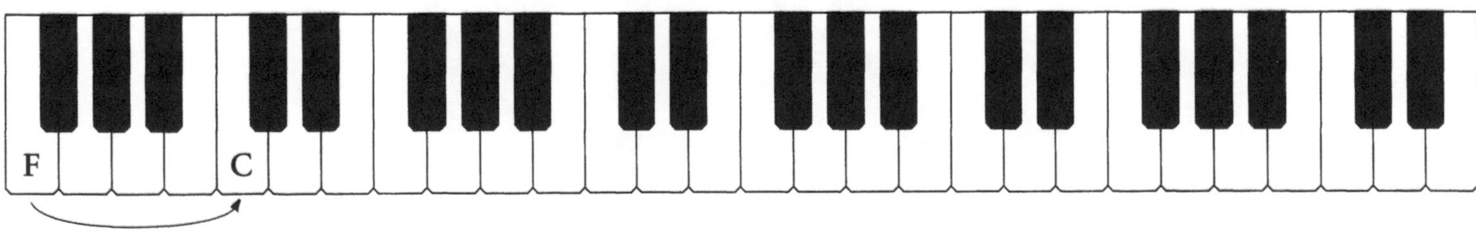

4. Starting on the lowest C: say letter names going up by 5ths.
say letter names going up by 4ths.
say letter names going up by 3rds.

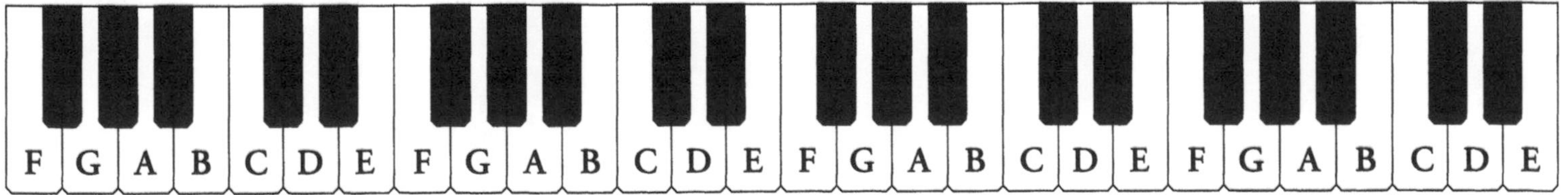

Use with pages 32-37 of Level B
FINGERCIZE NO. 8

1
f—p
5

Zoo Notes

1. In each animal's name, circle the letters that are in the musical alphabet.
2. For each circled letter, draw the notes on the staff. Use quarter notes.

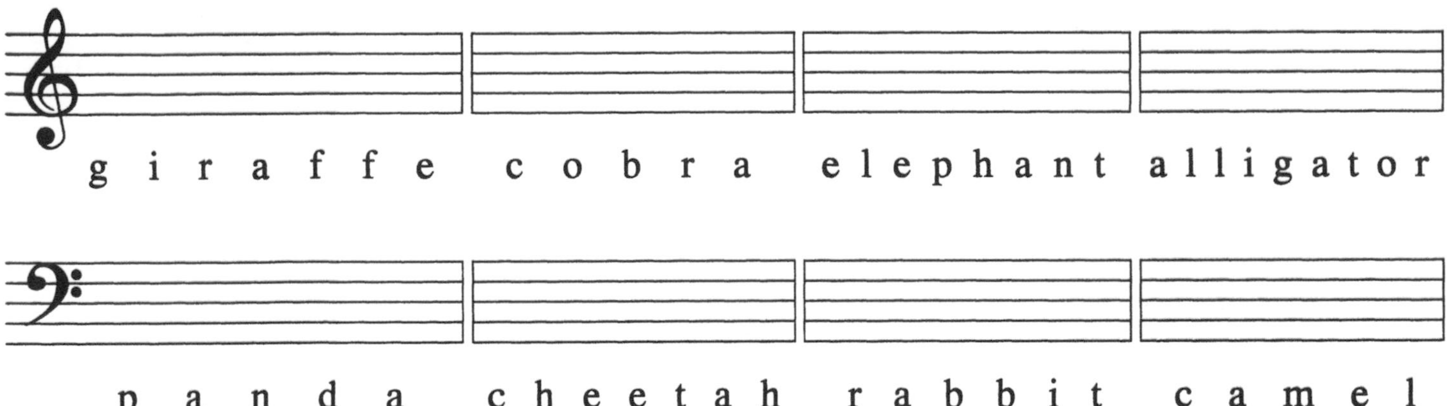

Ear Training

1. Use the first few notes of the songs to remember how each interval sounds.
2. Listen as your teacher plays one of the intervals. Can you name the interval?

2nds
Jesus, Jesus, Rest Your Head (page 22, Level B)

2nd

3rds
Haydn's Surprise (page 18, Level B)

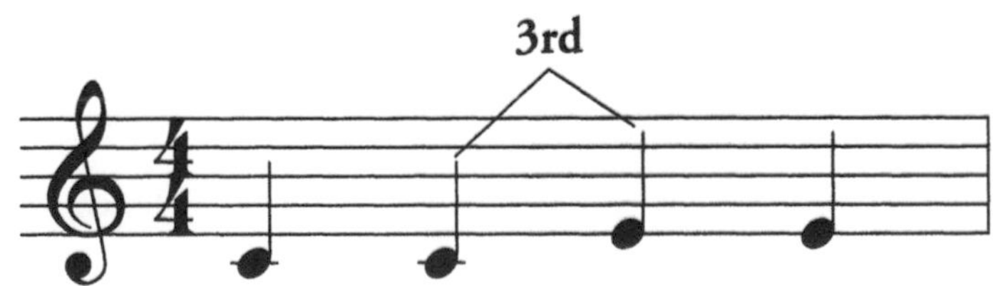

4ths
Jonah (page 28, Level B)

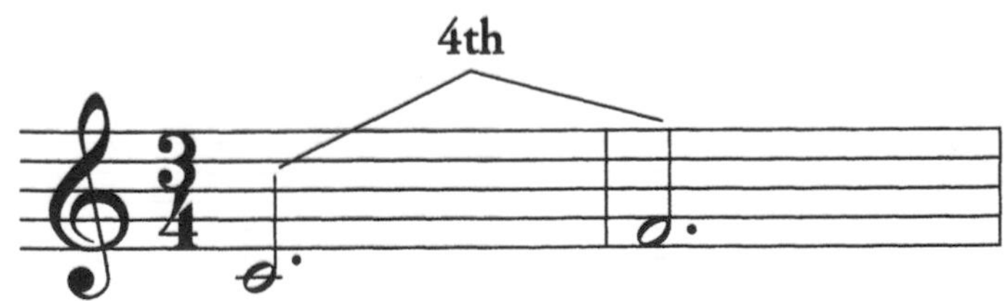

5ths
Sound the Trumpet! (page 32, Level B)

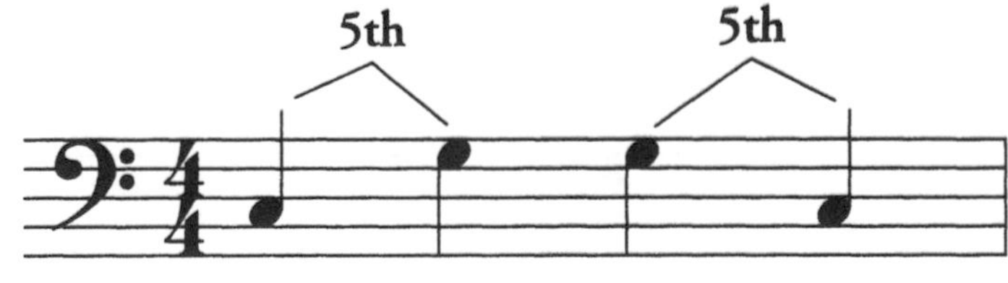

Your teacher will play each interval melodically and harmonically.

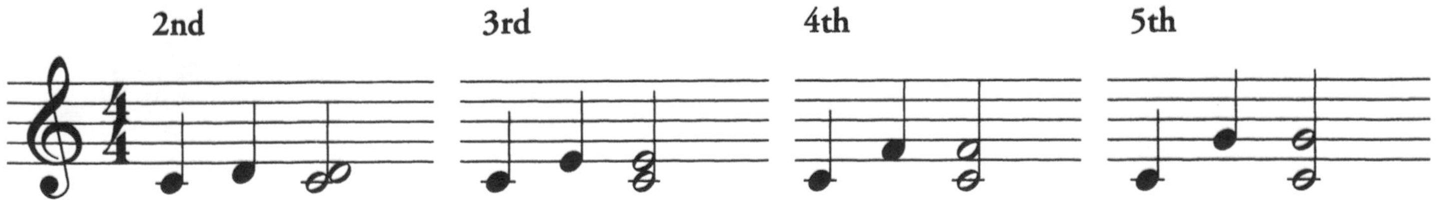

The Damper Pedal

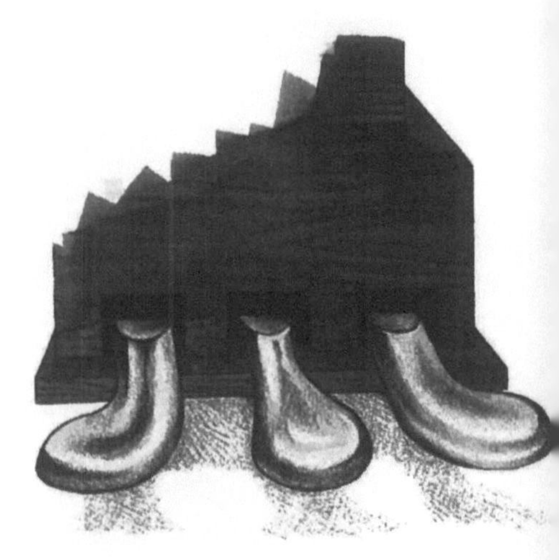

The **damper** or **sustaining pedal** is on the *right*. To hold tones, press the pedal with the ball of your right foot. Keep your heel resting on the floor.

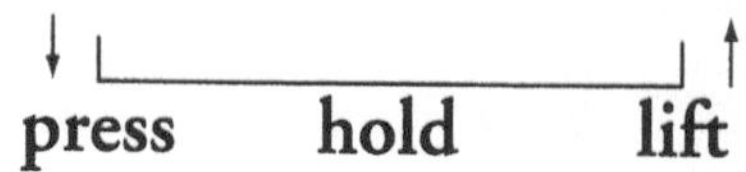

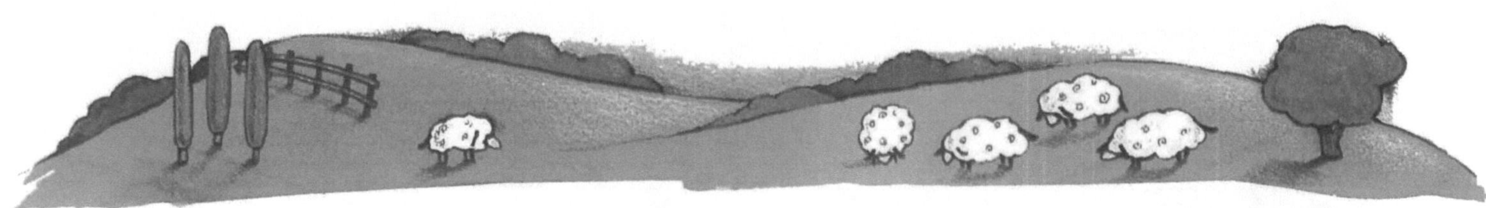

Spacewalk

Let's use our imagination and make up a song using intervals and the sustaining pedal.

- While holding down the pedal, play melodic 2nds, up or down from each of the pitches below.*
- You may play anywhere on the keyboard.
- You may play at any dynamic level or tempo.
- Try the same thing using melodic 3rds, 4ths, and 5ths.

D G C A

Now choose four new pitches and create your own outer space song.

- Use the intervals and dynamics that sound best to you.
- Give it your own title and write it in the box.

pitch names: ________ ________ ________ ________

*Teacher: Here is one possible realization.

Two Eighth Notes

Two eighth notes are equal to one quarter note.

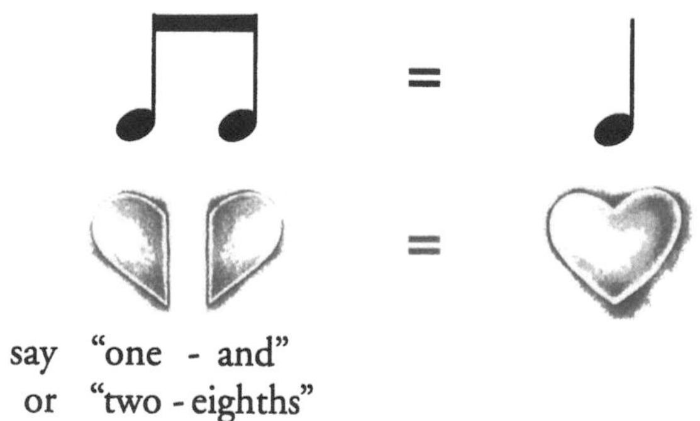

1. Complete the rhythm line by drawing two eighth notes or one quarter note.

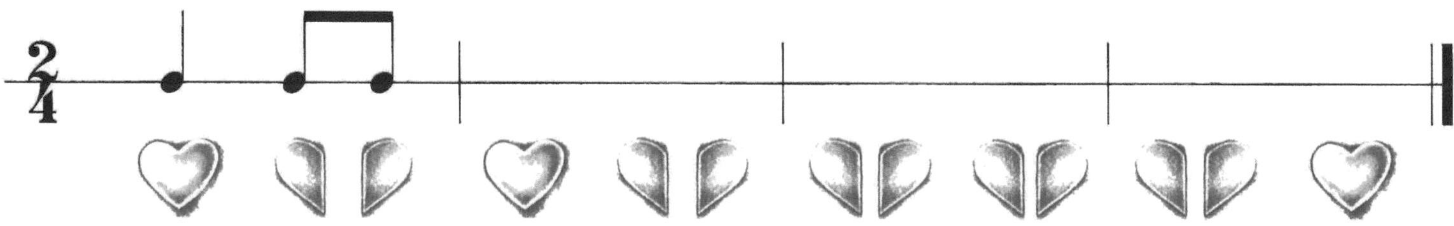

Rhythm Machine

2. For each quarter note (♩) clap your hands. For each two-eighth-note pair (♫), pat your lap. Practice each line three times every day until you can go really fast with no mistakes.

Quarter Splits

1. Rewrite each quarter note example as two eighth notes. Then write the number of beats.

2. Complete the line below with two eighths in each empty beat. Play each line.

3. Draw bar lines in the correct places for each line. Draw a double bar at the end. Use the time signature as your guide!

Victory March

You have been hired to play for the award ceremony at the Animal Olympics.

1. Write the correct *tempo* for each contestant.
2. Play the *Victory March* in the correct tempo as the trophy is given to each contestant.
3. Draw your own animal for the winner of the gymnastic event. Choose a *tempo.*

New Dynamic Signs

A New Dynamic Duo in the Middle of It!

You have already learned that ***p*** or *piano* means soft and ***f*** or *forte* means loud. Two new dynamic signs between ***p*** and ***f*** are ***mp*** and ***mf***.

p	***mp***	***mf***	***f***
piano	*mezzo piano*	*mezzo forte*	*forte*
or soft	or medium soft	or medium loud	or loud

Dynamic Scramble

1. Draw lines matching each dynamic sign to its name and meaning.

p •	• *mezzo piano* •	• medium loud
mp •	• *forte* •	• soft
mf •	• *piano* •	• medium soft
f •	• *mezzo forte* •	• loud

2. Write ***p***, ***mp***, ***mf***, or ***f*** in the box in each measure of the song to match the choir angel.
3. Play, observing the dynamics.

Wake-Up Call!

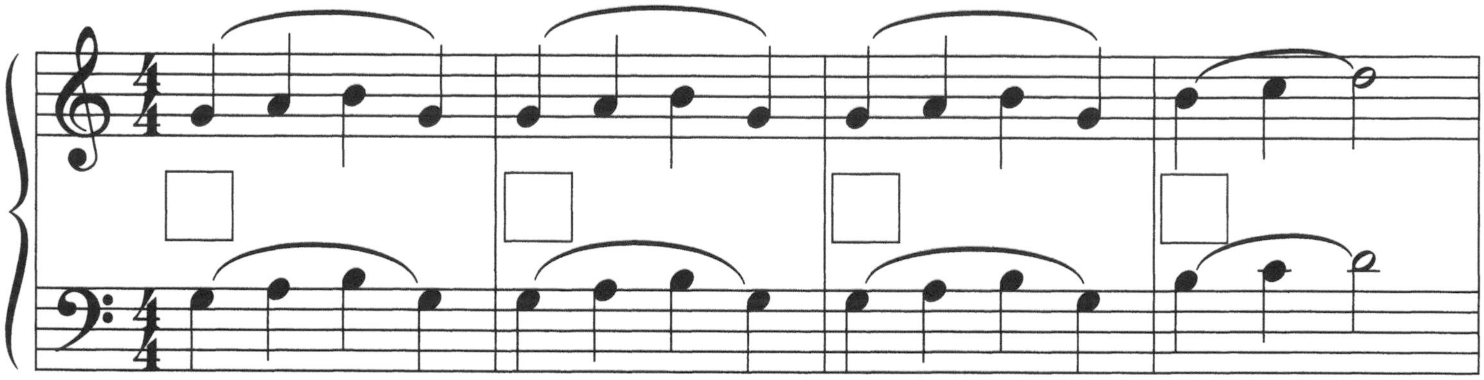

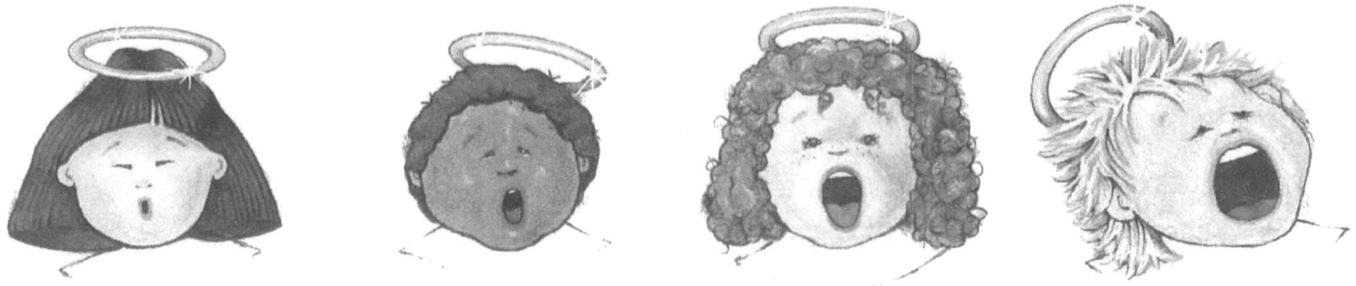

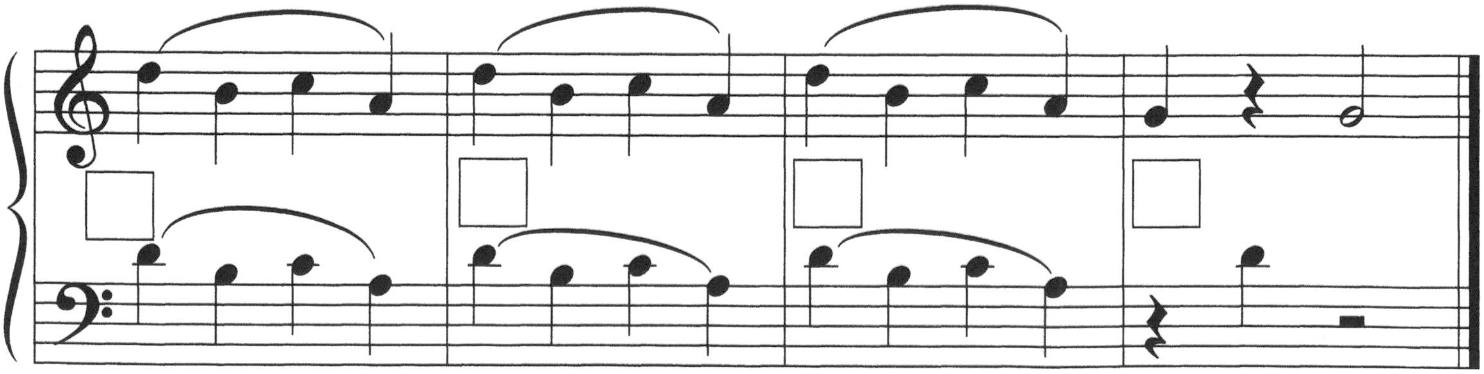

FINGERCIZE NO. 10

1
p
mp
mf
f
1
5

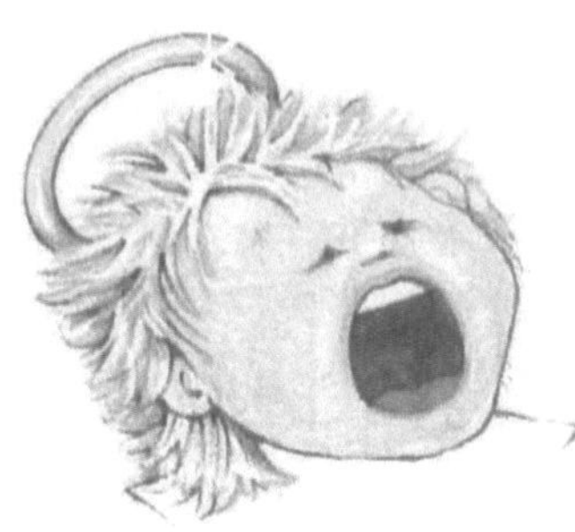

f
mf
mp rit.
p

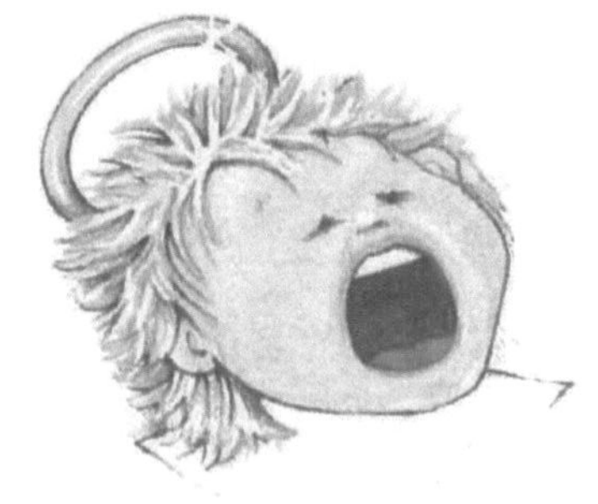

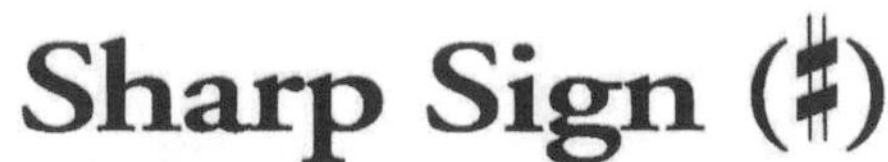

Sharp Sign (♯)

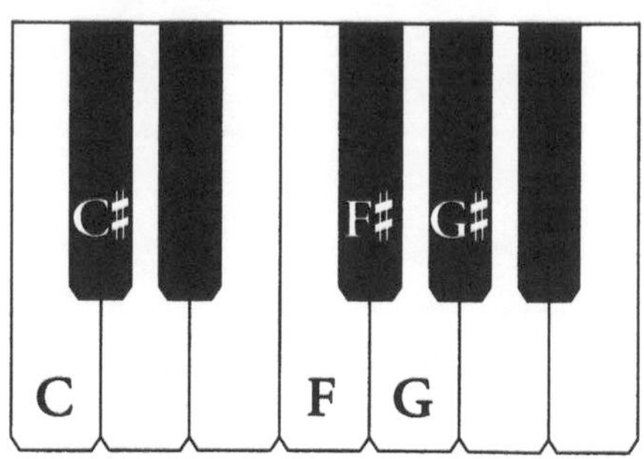

A **sharp sign (♯)** means to play the next key to the right. Sharped notes are usually on black keys, but they can also be on white keys.

Sharp Skills

1. Draw a sharp sign on the correct key on each keyboard.
2. Name the sharped keys

C♯

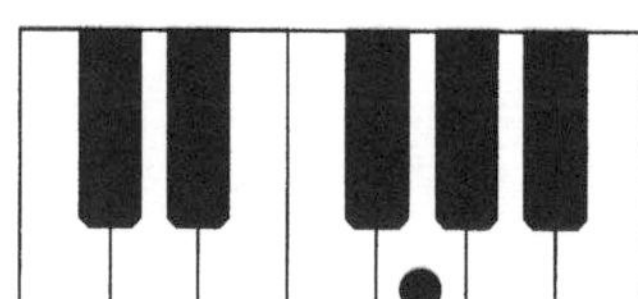

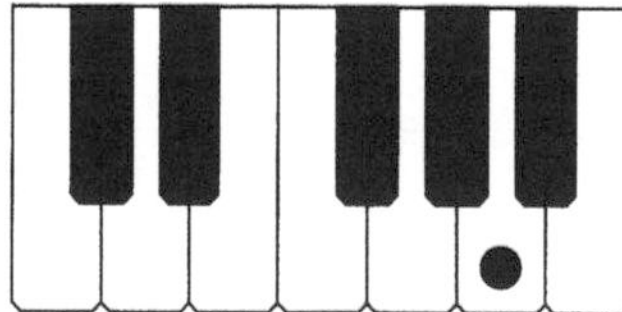

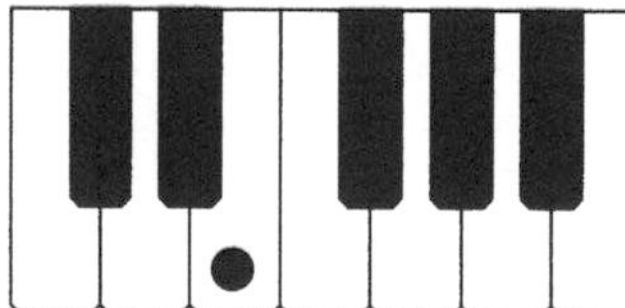

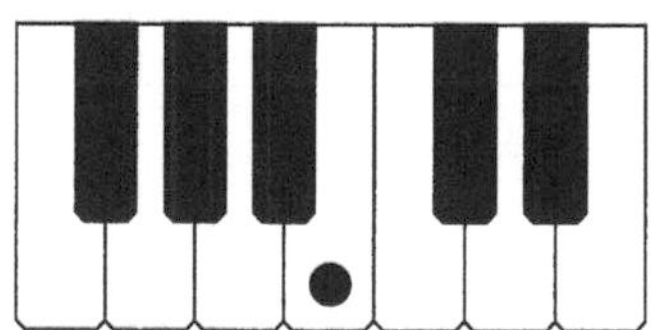

Sharps are drawn before the note on the same line or space as the note head.

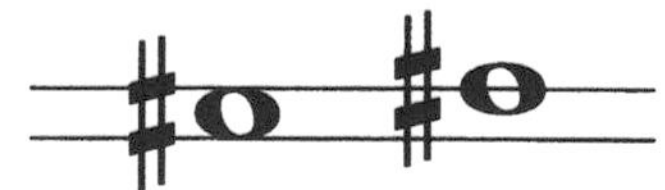

3. Draw a sharp sign for each note.
4. Name each note. Then play the note on your keyboard.

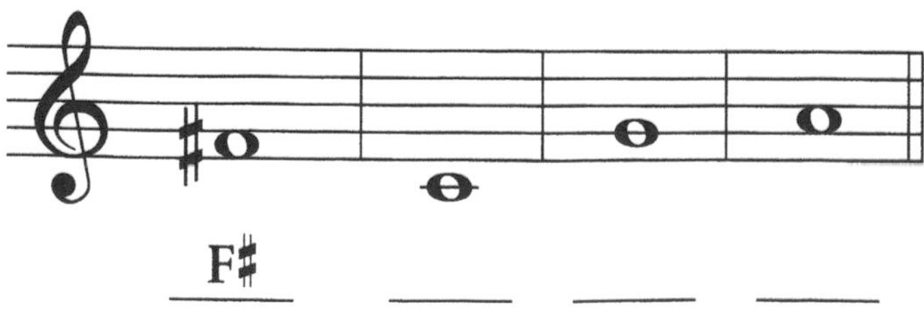

F♯ ____ ____ ____

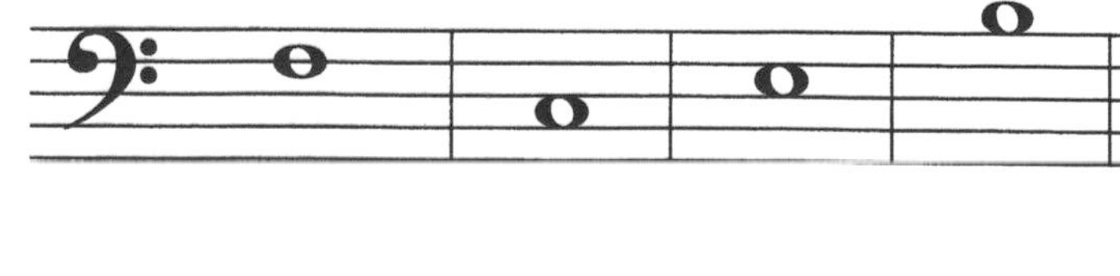

____ ____ ____ ____

5. Name the sharp, then
6. Draw the note on the staff using a whole note.

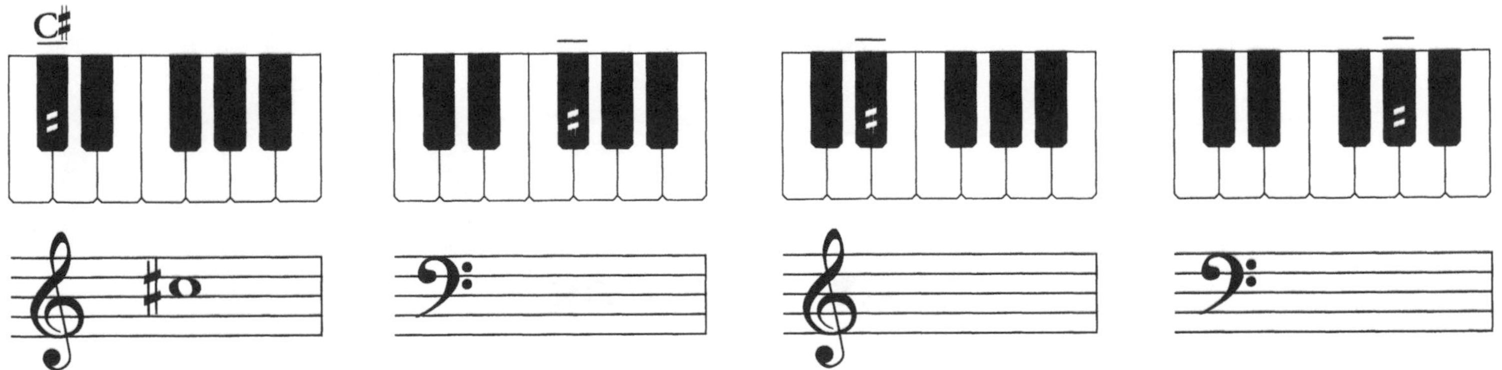

7. Find the sharps in *Fingercize No. 11.* What two sharp keys do you use?
____and____
8. Draw a sharp sign on each of these keys on this keyboard →
9. Play *Fingercize No. 11.*

Fingercize No. 11

mp *mf* *f*

New Dynamic Signs

Crescendo (cresc.)	*Diminuendo (dim.)*
play gradually louder	play gradually softer

Ear Training

1. Listen as your teacher plays each line using a *crescendo* or *diminuendo.* Draw a *crescendo* or *diminuendo* sign to show how your teacher played it.

2. Draw a *crescendo* or *diminuendo* sign next to each picture to show how it would sound.

a. A parade coming toward you. ___________

b. An airplane leaving the airport. ___________

c. The school bus coming to your stop. ___________

d. Turning your radio down. ___________

Staccato

Staccato means to play the note short and separated from the note after it. *Staccato* playing is shown with a dot over or under the note.

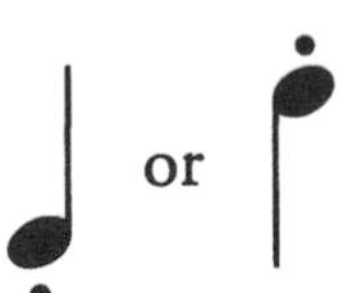

Playing Staccato

1. Play the line below with short separated sounds. Try not to "punch" the keys.

2. Play *Fingercize No. 12.* Notice that you will need to play both *legato* (connected) and *staccato.*

FINGERCIZE NO. 12

1

p

mf

5

p

mf

Flat Sign (♭)

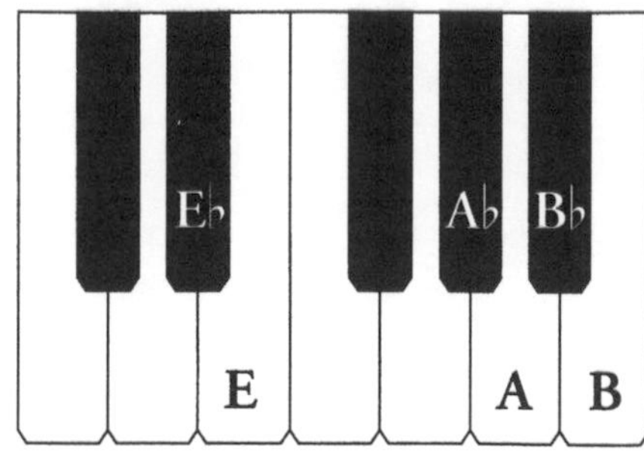

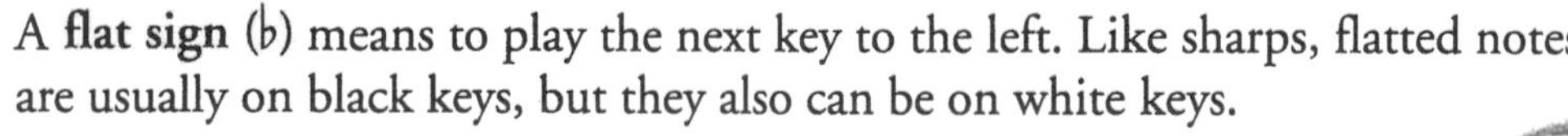

A **flat sign** (♭) means to play the next key to the left. Like sharps, flatted notes are usually on black keys, but they also can be on white keys.

Flat Skills

1. Draw a flat sign on the correct key on each keyboard.
2. Name the flatted key.

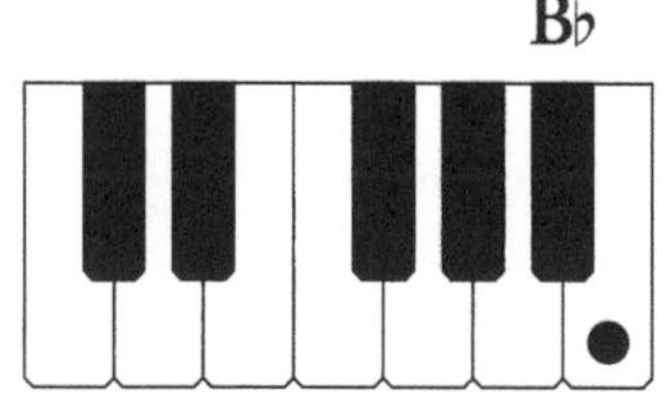

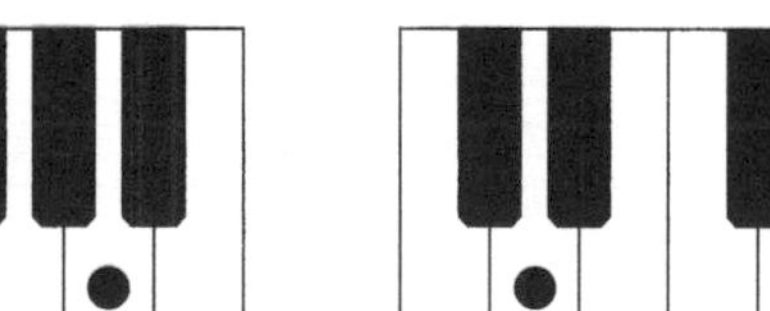

Flats are drawn before the note on the same line or space as the note head.

3. Draw a flat sign before each note.
4. Name each note. Then play the note on your keyboard.

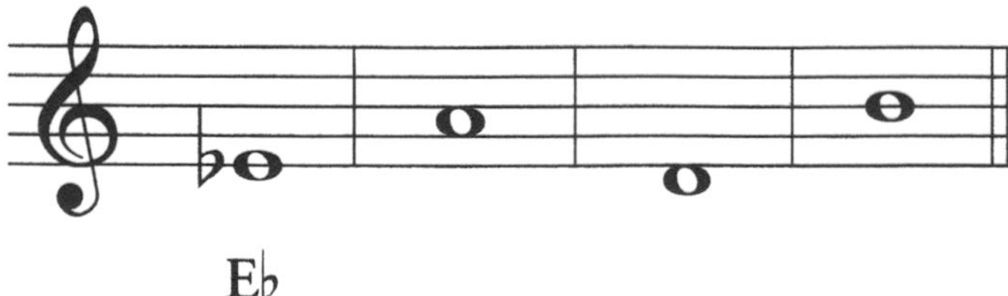

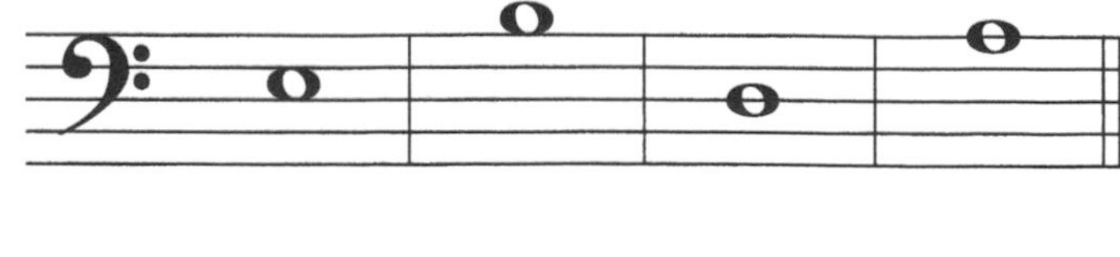

5. Name the flat, then
6. Draw the note, using a whole note.

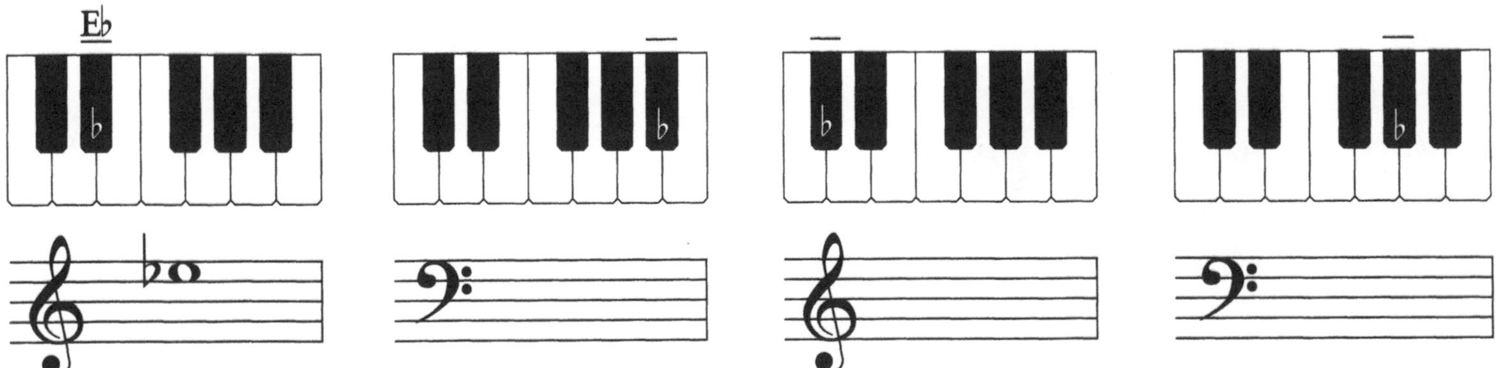

7. Find the flats in *Fingercize No. 13.* What two flat keys do you use?
   ____and____.
8. Draw a flat sign on each of these keys on this keyboard →
9. Play *Fingercize No. 13.*

Fingercize No. 13

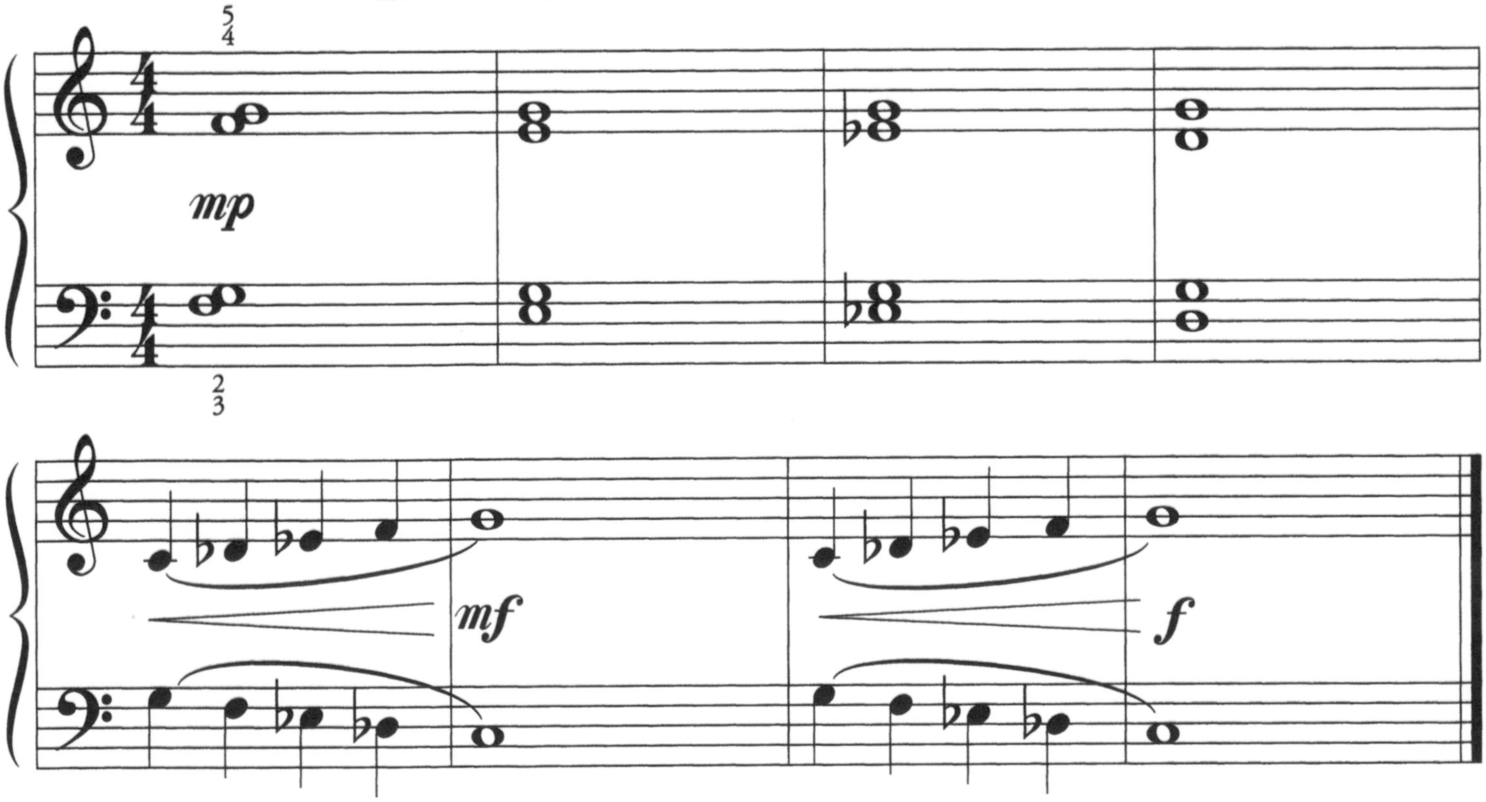

Ear Training

Can you tell if a note is going sharp or flat? Listen as your teacher plays a note and its sharp or flat*. If the note goes down, circle the flat sign. If the note goes up, circle the sharp sign.

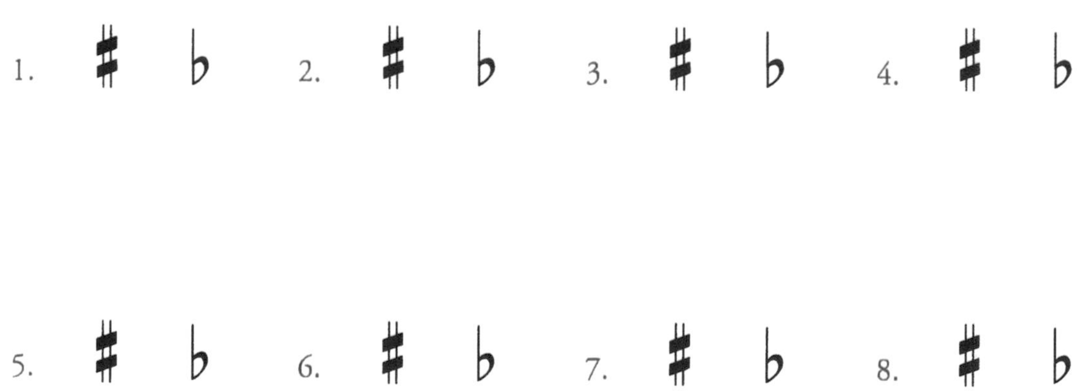

Now listen as your teacher plays a note and its sharp or flat. This time, *call out* either "sharp" or "flat." See how quickly you can call out the answer after your teacher plays each pair of notes.

*Teacher: play examples melodically such as F, F♯ or C, C♯, etc.

Final Review

Intervals

1. Draw a whole note above the note given to make harmonic intervals.
2. Write the names of the notes below the staff.

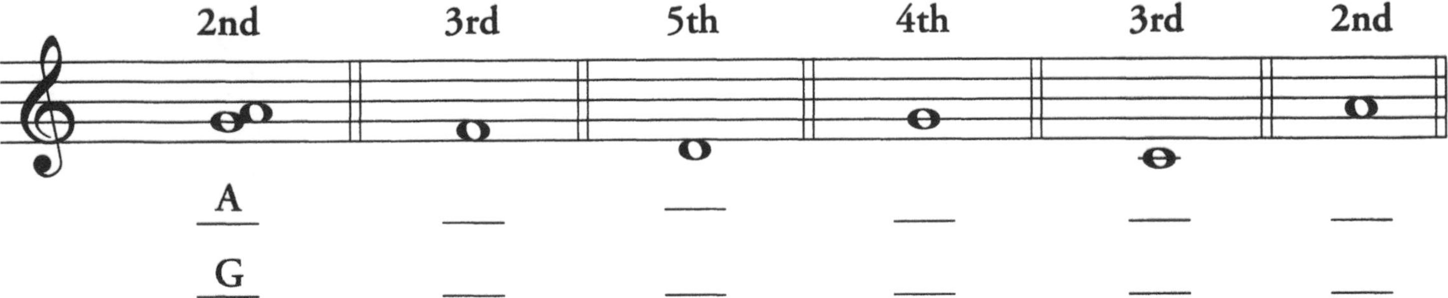

3. Draw a half note after the note given to make melodic intervals. Follow the direction of each arrow.
4. Write the names of the notes below the staff.

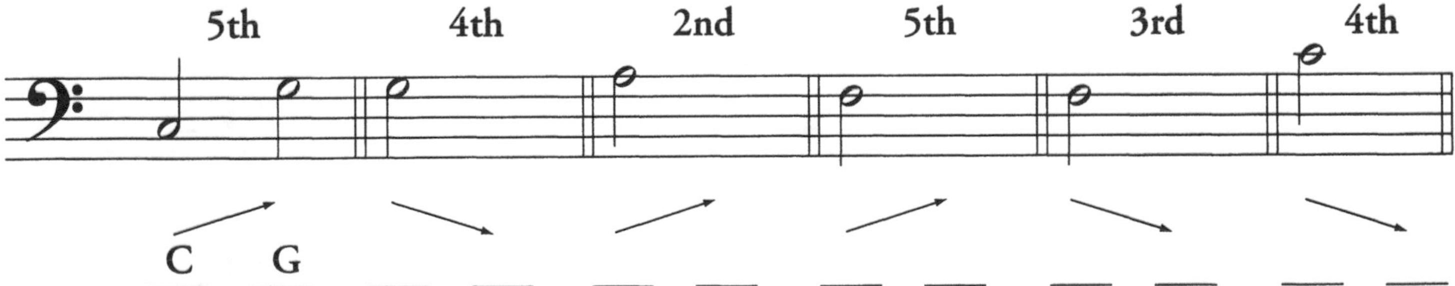

V. I. P. Drill

5. Draw the V. I. P. notes low C, F, middle C, G, and high C on the grand staff.
6. Write the names of the V. I. P. notes on the keyboard below the staff.

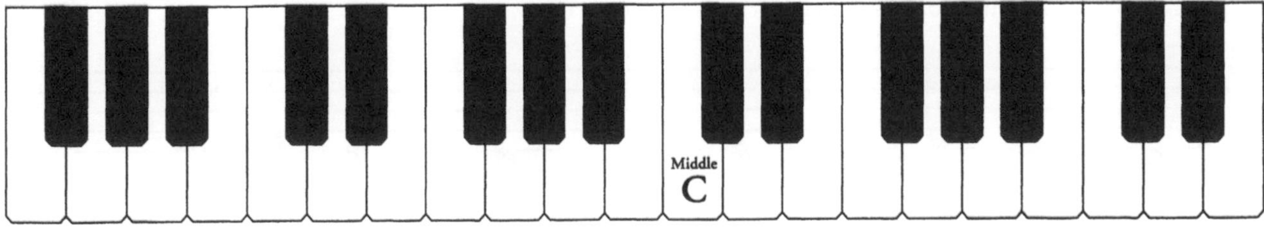

7. Draw lines connecting the dots to match the correct answers.

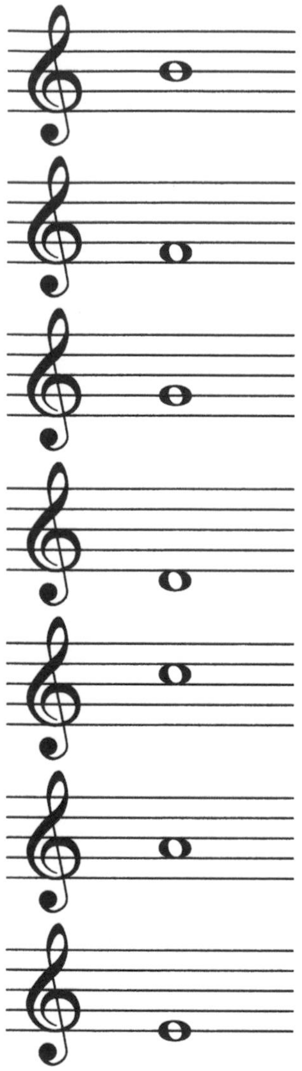

G

B

D

F

A

C

E

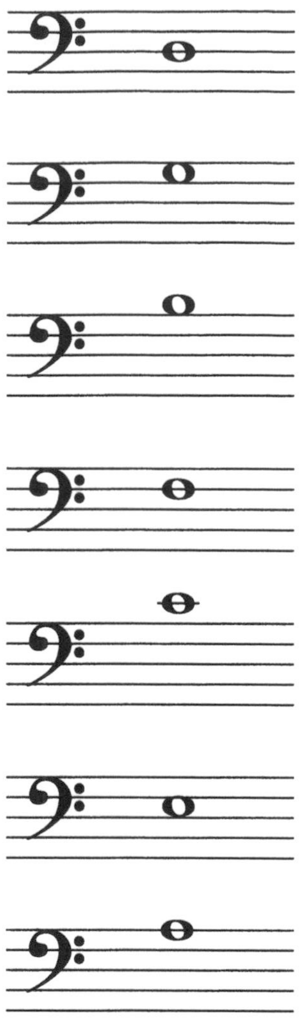

8. Write *legato* or *staccato* under the correct staff. Play each line.

_______________ _______________

9. A slur means to play_______________

10. Write the correct number of beats below the tied notes. Play.

beats beats beats

11. Complete each measure with *either* a quarter note or two eighth notes.
12. Count the rhythm. For each quarter note, clap your hands. For each two-eighth-note pair, pat your lap.

13. Draw lines connecting the dots to match the correct answers.

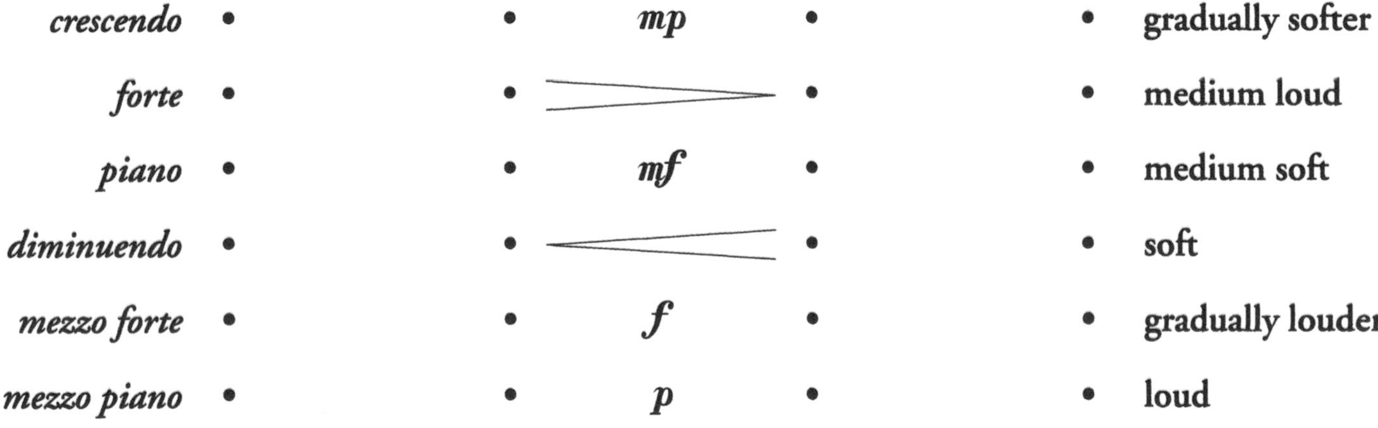

14. Write the name of each note on the line below it; then draw a sharp or flat on the correct key.

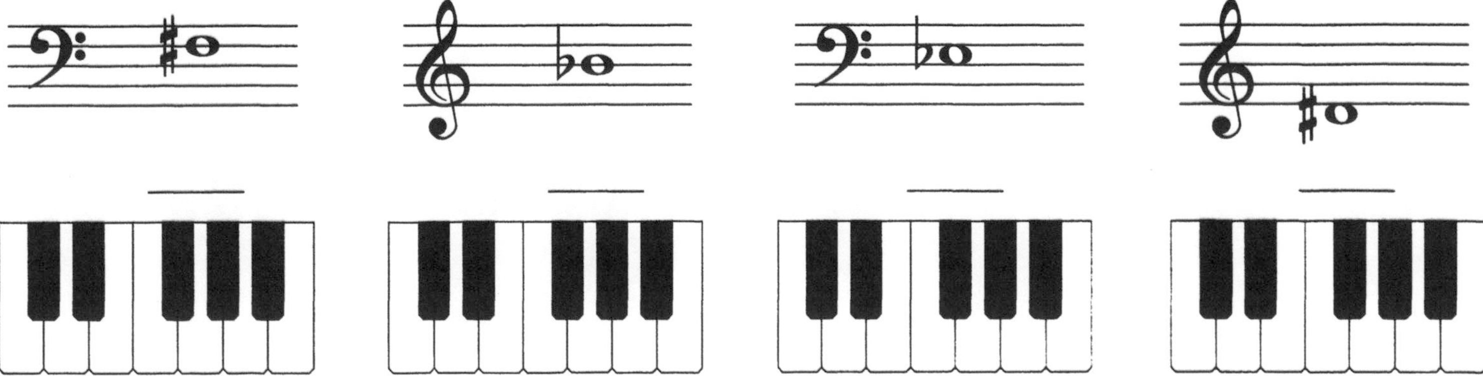